COPENHAGE

ULTIMATE TRAVEL GUIDE 2025

Discover the Best of Copenhagen: History, Culture, Insider Tips, Hidden Gems, and Must-See Attractions

BY

LUCIE WINGARD

Copyright Notice

© 2024 by Lucie Wingard. All rights reserved.

Lucie Wingard, an esteemed traveler and prolific author of numerous travel guides, holds exclusive rights to this publication. This guidebook, including all text, photographs, maps, and illustrations contained herein, is protected under the United States and international copyright laws.

No part of this book may be reproduced, distributed, or transmitted in any form or by any means, including photocopying, recording, or other electronic or mechanical methods, without the prior written permission of the author, except in the case of brief quotations embodied in critical reviews and certain other noncommercial uses permitted by copyright law. For permission requests, please write to the author via the author's central page.

TABLE OF CONTENTS

Copyright..1
My Experience In Copenhagen...5
About This Guide...7

Chapter 1 Introduction To Copenhagen..11
1.1 Welcome To Copenhagen...11
1.2 History And Culture..13
1.3 Geography, Climate & Best Time To Visit......................................15

Chapter 2 Accommodation Options..19
2.1 Luxury Hotels And Boutique Hotels..20
2.2 Budget-Friendly Options (Hostels, Guesthouses)............................22
2.3 Vacation Rentals And Apartments...25
2.4 Unique Stays: Historic Buildings And Design Hotels.....................27
2.5 Local Neighborhoods And Areas To Stay.......................................30

Chapter 3 Transportation...33
3.1 Getting To Copenhagen..33
3.2 Public Transportation Options (Metro, Bus, Train)........................35
3.3 Taxi And Ride-Hailing Services..37
3.4 Cycling And Bike-Friendly Infrastructure......................................39
3.5 Car Rentals And Driving Tips...42
3.6 Airport Transfers And Shuttle Services..45

Chapter 4 Top 10 Attractions & Hidden Gems....................................47
4.1 Tivoli Gardens And Amusement Park...48
4.2 Nyhavn Harbour And Colourful Houses...50
4.3 Amalienborg Palace And Royal Guard...52
4.4 The Little Mermaid And Waterfront...54
4.5 National Museum Of Denmark And History..................................56

4.6 Christiansborg Palace And Parliament..58
4.7 Rosenborg Castle And Gardens.. 60
4.8 Vesterbro And Meatpacking District..63
4.9 Østerbro And Parken Stadium...65
4.10 Frederiksberg And Gardens..67
4.11 Outdoor Activities And Adventures...69
4.12 Guided Tours And Recommended Tour Operators......................72

Chapter 5 Practical Information And Guidance...................................75
5.1 Maps And Navigation... 75
5.2 Four Days Itinerary... 77
5.3 Essential Packing List.. 80
5.4 Setting Your Travel Budget..83
5.5 Visa Requirements And Entry Procedures..86
5.6 Safety Tips And Emergency Contacts..88
5.7 Currency Exchange And Banking Services...................................... 91
5.8 Language, Communication And Useful Phrases..............................94
5.9 Shopping In Copenhagen... 96
5.10 Health And Wellness Centers...99
5.11 Useful Websites, Mobile Apps And Online Resources............. 101
5.12 Internet Access And Connectivity...103
5.13 Visitor Centers And Tourist Assistance.......................................106

Chapter 6 Gastronomic Delights..109
6.1 Dining Options And Top Restaurants... 109
6.2 Danish Cuisine And Local Specialties (Smørrebrød, Flæskesteg)...............112
6.3 Street Food And Markets..114
6.4 Coffee Culture And Cafes.. 116
6.5 Cooking Classes And Culinary Workshops....................................118
6.6 Nightlife And Entertainment..120
6.7 Craft Beer And Breweries.. 122

Chapter 7 Day Trips And Excursions...........125
7.1 Roskilde And Viking Ship Museum...........126
7.2 Kronborg Castle And Helsingør...........129
7.3 Hillerød And Frederiksborg Castle...........132
7.4 Malmö And Sweden...........135
7.5 Louisiana Museum Of Modern Art And Sculpture Park...........137

Chapter 8 Events And Festivals...........140
8.1 Copenhagen Jazz Festival (July)...........140
8.2 Tivoli Gardens Christmas Market (December)...........142
8.3 Copenhagen Pride And Parade (August)...........144
8.4 Copenhagen Marathon And Running Events (May)...........146
8.5 Strøget Christmas Lights And Shopping (December)...........149
Conclusion And Recommendations...........152

MY EXPERIENCE IN COPENHAGEN

As someone who has traversed countless cities around the world, few have captivated me as deeply as Copenhagen. From the moment I set foot in this enchanting Danish capital, I felt an immediate connection—a sense that this was a place where history and innovation coexisted in perfect harmony. The first thing that struck me about Copenhagen was its effortless simplicity. The air was crisp and refreshing, carrying a faint whisper of the sea. Arriving at Kastrup Airport was a seamless experience, a testament to the Danish reputation for efficiency. The short metro ride into the city offered a tantalizing preview of what lay ahead: colorful townhouses along the canals, sleek modern architecture, and a bicycle-friendly culture that felt refreshingly different. As I stepped out into the city center, the iconic Nyhavn greeted me like a scene from a postcard, instantly setting the tone for my journey.

Nyhavn, with its kaleidoscope of brightly painted facades lining the tranquil canal, was more than just a tourist hotspot—it was a living, breathing piece of history. Once a bustling port, it now serves as a vibrant gathering place filled with lively cafes and restaurants. I found myself sitting at one of the waterfront tables, sipping a steaming cup of coffee while soaking in the picturesque view. The gentle clinking of boat masts in the harbor and the laughter of locals and tourists alike created a warm, welcoming ambiance. It was here, staring at the timeless beauty of Nyhavn, that I began to understand why Hans Christian Andersen called Copenhagen home. One of the most delightful ways to explore Copenhagen is by bicycle. Renting a bike felt like embracing the very soul of the city. The extensive cycling infrastructure, with its dedicated bike lanes and friendly etiquette, made it easy to navigate the streets like a local. As I pedaled through neighborhoods, past the serene lakes and along the harborfront, I marveled at how seamlessly Copenhagen balances its old-world charm with contemporary living.

My cycling adventures led me to Freetown Christiania, a self-declared autonomous neighborhood unlike any other. This colorful enclave is a haven for artists, dreamers, and free spirits. Wandering through its graffiti-covered streets and eclectic markets felt like stepping into another dimension—a stark yet fascinating contrast to Copenhagen's otherwise orderly demeanor. The creativity and individuality on display here spoke volumes about the city's open-mindedness and progressive spirit. Another highlight of my trip was Tivoli Gardens, the world-renowned amusement park that has been enchanting visitors since 1843. Entering Tivoli felt like stepping into a whimsical wonderland. The fairy lights twinkled above cobblestone pathways, and the sound of live music floated through the air. I spent hours exploring its gardens, savoring traditional Danish pastries, and even daring to ride some of its vintage attractions. As night fell, Tivoli transformed into a magical spectacle, and I couldn't help but feel a childlike wonder that I hadn't experienced in years.

No travel experience is complete without delving into the local cuisine, and Copenhagen's food scene did not disappoint. Danish gastronomy is an art form, and the city's emphasis on fresh, local ingredients was evident in every bite. From savoring traditional smørrebrød at a charming café to sampling Nordic delicacies at Torvehallerne food market, every meal was a celebration of flavor and craftsmanship. Torvehallerne, with its bustling stalls offering everything from artisanal cheeses to freshly baked pastries, was a sensory delight. Copenhagen's historical treasures are equally captivating. Amalienborg Palace, the royal family's residence, exudes an understated elegance that reflects Denmark's refined sense of tradition. Watching the ceremonial changing of the guard here was a humbling experience, a reminder of the city's rich heritage. Rosenborg Castle, with its stunning gardens and opulent interiors, offered another glimpse into the royal past. Walking through its halls and admiring the crown jewels, I felt transported to a bygone era of grandeur.

As my time in Copenhagen drew to a close, I found myself reflecting on the city's unique charm. Standing by the harbor at sunset, with the iconic Little Mermaid statue gazing wistfully at the water, I felt a profound sense of peace. Copenhagen isn't just a place you visit—it's a place you feel, a city that wraps itself around you and leaves an imprint on your soul. Copenhagen's magic lies in its ability to balance the old and the new, the tranquil and the vibrant. It's a city where you can lose yourself in the pages of history and then find yourself in the energy of its contemporary culture. For me, it wasn't just another destination; it was an experience, a story, and a memory that I'll cherish forever.

ABOUT THIS GUIDE

This guide is your ultimate companion to navigate the city and make the most of your visit. Whether you're a first-time traveler or a seasoned explorer, this guide is designed to offer you a deep dive into all that Copenhagen has to offer, providing you with practical tips, hidden gems, and essential resources for your adventure.

Maps and Navigation

One of the first challenges visitors face when traveling to a new city is figuring out how to navigate it. In Copenhagen Comprehensive Guide, we cover everything you need to know about getting around this beautiful city. Copenhagen is a well-organized city with a robust and reliable public transportation system. The guide includes detailed maps of the city center, covering the most popular districts, key landmarks, and hidden treasures. We'll walk you through the best methods of transportation, including the metro, buses, and bicycles – a quintessential Copenhagen experience. With an extensive network of cycle paths, Copenhagen is one of the most bicycle-friendly cities in the world. You'll find clear instructions on where to rent bikes, how to navigate the cycle lanes, and the benefits of cycling through the city.

Accommodation Options

Finding the perfect place to stay in Copenhagen is made easy with our detailed breakdown of accommodation options. From luxurious 5-star hotels to cozy boutique guesthouses, there's something to suit every traveler's budget and preference. For those seeking luxury, we explore the city's most opulent hotels, offering panoramic views of the cityscape, world-class amenities, and impeccable service. Budget-conscious travelers are also well catered for, with a selection of affordable hostels, budget hotels, and charming Airbnbs, many located in central areas, making it easy to access all the major attractions. Moreover, we highlight mid-range hotels that offer excellent value for money and provide practical recommendations based on location, amenities, and guest reviews. Whether you're staying in the bustling city center or a quiet, picturesque neighborhood, you'll find a comfortable place to rest and recharge in this comprehensive guide.

Transportation

Copenhagen's transportation system is efficient, well-connected, and easy to navigate. The guide covers the city's public transit options, including the metro,

S-train, buses, and water buses, offering detailed information on routes, schedules, and ticketing systems. For those flying into Copenhagen, we'll provide step-by-step instructions on how to get from Copenhagen Airport to the city center, whether you prefer taking a taxi, the metro, or the Airport Bus. You'll also find information on the Copenhagen Card, a travel pass that offers unlimited use of public transportation and free entry to many of the city's top attractions.

Top Attractions
Copenhagen is a city brimming with fascinating attractions, and our guide provides a comprehensive list of must-see sights. From the world-famous Tivoli Gardens, one of the oldest amusement parks in the world, to the iconic Little Mermaid statue, there's no shortage of historic and cultural landmarks to explore. The guide also covers the city's impressive art museums, including the Louisiana Museum of Modern Art and the National Gallery of Denmark, as well as the vibrant Nyhavn harbor, known for its colorful buildings and lively atmosphere. For those interested in royal history, we take you through the Royal Palaces, such as Amalienborg Palace, and the magnificent Rosenborg Castle, home to Denmark's crown jewels. We don't just stop at the typical tourist spots; we also delve into off-the-beaten-path attractions like the alternative Christiania neighborhood, the Copenhagen Opera House, and the fascinating National Museum of Denmark.

Practical Information and Travel Resources
To make your visit to Copenhagen as smooth as possible, we provide all the practical information you might need. This includes important tips on currency (Danish krone), language (Danish, with many people fluent in English), and essential emergency contacts such as local police, hospitals, and embassies. You'll also find information on SIM cards, Wi-Fi availability, and mobile apps that can help you make the most of your time in the city. Whether you need to find the nearest ATM, locate a restaurant, or check the weather forecast, our guide ensures you'll be well-prepared.

Culinary Delights
Copenhagen is a food lover's paradise, with its world-renowned culinary scene, which has earned the city Michelin stars and international recognition. The guide delves into the best dining spots in the city, from fine dining establishments like Noma (often cited as one of the world's best restaurants) to

cozy cafes serving traditional Danish pastries. We provide a comprehensive breakdown of the city's food districts, highlighting areas such as Torvehallerne, a food market offering a wide variety of local produce and gourmet delicacies, and Vesterbro, known for its trendy eateries. Additionally, we feature the city's beloved smørrebrød (open-faced sandwiches) and tips on where to try these iconic dishes, as well as hidden gems for international cuisine and vegetarian/vegan options. The guide also provides information on food tours, where you can taste your way through Copenhagen's diverse culinary landscape.

Culture and Heritage
Copenhagen is steeped in rich cultural heritage, and this guide takes you on a journey through the city's history, traditions, and artistic achievements. From the royal history that permeates the city's palaces to the cultural institutions like the Royal Danish Theater, Copenhagen offers a fascinating exploration of Danish history. We also delve into the city's thriving modern cultural scene, from contemporary art galleries to street art in the Freetown Christiania district. Learn about Denmark's Viking roots, the city's role during the Age of Enlightenment, and the evolution of Copenhagen into a modern cosmopolitan hub.

Outdoor Activities and Adventures
Copenhagen is a city for adventurers and outdoor enthusiasts. This guide explores the many outdoor activities that you can enjoy, including kayaking along the canals, cycling around the city's many parks, and walking tours through Copenhagen's green spaces.For nature lovers, we recommend exploring the Frederiksberg Gardens or taking a boat tour along the city's canals. We also feature Copenhagen's stunning beaches, such as Amager Strandpark, perfect for swimming or a day of sunbathing during the summer months.

Shopping
Copenhagen is a fashion-forward city, offering a blend of international brands and local boutiques. The guide explores the best shopping districts, including the pedestrian-friendly Strøget, one of Europe's longest shopping streets, and the stylish Vesterbro district, where you can find independent designers and quirky shops. If you're a fan of Scandinavian design, we provide a list of shops where you can pick up homeware, fashion, and accessories by iconic Danish designers like HAY and Georg Jensen. Additionally, we feature Copenhagen's design markets and concept stores, where you can discover unique, handcrafted items.

Day Trips and Excursions
Copenhagen's central location makes it a perfect base for exploring the wider region of Zealand. This guide includes detailed information on day trips and excursions to nearby destinations, such as the historic town of Roskilde, home to the Viking Ship Museum, or the fairytale-like Frederiksborg Castle. We also cover day trips to the picturesque town of Helsingør, famous for its Kronborg Castle (the setting of Shakespeare's Hamlet), and the charming seaside village of Gilleleje. Whether you prefer history, nature, or art, this guide offers a variety of options for your day trips from Copenhagen.

Entertainment and Nightlife
Copenhagen has a vibrant nightlife scene, and this guide helps you navigate it with ease. From trendy cocktail bars and underground clubs to cozy pubs and live music venues, the city offers a diverse range of options for night owls. The guide includes recommendations for bars in the hip Nørrebro district, a lively area known for its multicultural vibe, as well as high-end cocktail lounges in the heart of the city. If you're looking for live music, we highlight venues such as the Copenhagen Jazzhouse and Vega, one of the city's most iconic concert venues.

CHAPTER 1
INTRODUCTION TO COPENHAGEN

1.1 Welcome to Copenhagen

Welcome to Copenhagen, a city where history, innovation, and culture converge in a seamless blend that captivates the heart and the mind. From the moment you arrive, you'll sense the energy of a place that celebrates its past while embracing the future with open arms. It's a city where you can walk down streets lined with colorful buildings, savor world-class food, and explore centuries-old palaces, all within a short stroll of each other. Copenhagen is a place that invites you to linger and discover, offering something for every traveler—whether you're a history enthusiast, a lover of art, or simply someone in search of a new adventure. The city's charm is immediately apparent when you set foot in the heart of the city. Located at the eastern edge of the island of Zealand, Copenhagen's central district feels intimate yet vibrant, a place where modern cafes and shops coexist with landmarks that have stood the test of time. The contrast is striking, yet harmonious. One of the first places you'll encounter is the iconic Nyhavn, located just a few steps from Kongens Nytorv Square. The canal here, flanked by buildings painted in cheerful hues, evokes a sense of nostalgia and wonder. Once a bustling port filled with merchant ships, Nyhavn has transformed into a hub of culture and leisure. Today, it's lined with lively restaurants, each serving up Danish specialties that will have you craving more. As you stroll along the water's edge, the hum of conversation and the sound of boats gently bobbing in the harbor create a peaceful yet vibrant atmosphere. It's hard not to be drawn in by the charm of this place, which has inspired artists and writers, including Hans Christian Andersen, who called Nyhavn home for a time.

Just a short distance from Nyhavn, the heart of Copenhagen beats at the famous pedestrian street, Strøget. This bustling thoroughfare is home to everything from high-end boutiques to charming local shops. It's the perfect place to experience Copenhagen's mix of contemporary design and traditional Scandinavian style. As you wander through Strøget, you'll encounter beautiful squares and historic churches, like the Church of Our Lady, which offer a glimpse into the city's rich history. But Copenhagen is not a city that clings too tightly to its past—it's a place that invites change and innovation. This is evident in the architectural marvels scattered throughout the city, like the modernist design of the Danish National Bank or the striking curves of the Opera House, located just across the harbor in the neighborhood of Holmen. Of course, no visit to Copenhagen would be complete without experiencing its food culture. The city has garnered international acclaim for its culinary scene, and rightfully so. Copenhagen's restaurants offer an array of flavors, from casual eateries serving classic Danish fare to Michelin-starred dining experiences that showcase the best of Nordic cuisine. A visit to the Torvehallerne food market is a must for anyone who appreciates fresh, local produce. Located near Nørreport Station, this vibrant market is home to dozens of stalls offering everything from artisan cheeses and meats to freshly made pastries and gourmet street food. It's the perfect place to grab a quick bite or take your time sampling the best of Danish delicacies, like smørrebrød, the open-faced sandwich that's a staple of the local diet.

Copenhagen's commitment to sustainability and environmental responsibility is another aspect of the city that makes it stand out. Copenhagen has long been recognized as one of the greenest cities in the world, and it's easy to see why. The city's extensive cycling infrastructure makes it one of the best cities in the world for biking. With designated bike lanes running throughout the city, cycling is a natural and enjoyable way to get around. The city is also home to beautiful parks and green spaces like the King's Garden, which surrounds Rosenborg Castle, and Frederiksberg Gardens, where locals come to relax and enjoy nature. If you're in the mood for something more active, a bike ride along the harborfront will offer stunning views of the water and the city's modern skyline, as well as an up-close look at landmarks like the Copenhagen Opera House and the Little Mermaid statue. Copenhagen's historical richness is on full display in its royal palaces and museums. Amalienborg Palace, located in the Frederiksstaden district, is the residence of the Danish royal family, and a visit here will take you into the heart of Denmark's royal history. The changing of the guard ceremony, which takes place every day at noon, is a popular event for visitors. Rosenborg Castle, situated in the city center near the King's Garden, is another must-see. Home to the Danish crown jewels, this Renaissance-style castle offers a fascinating look at Denmark's royal past, complete with opulent rooms and impressive collections.

Yet, Copenhagen is not a city frozen in time. It is a place that thrives on creativity and innovation. A perfect example of this is the free-spirited community of Christiania, a self-proclaimed autonomous neighborhood located in the heart of the city. Founded in the early 1970s, Christiania has become an emblem of Copenhagen's openness and progressive spirit. The neighborhood is filled with colorful murals, quirky shops, and lively cafes, offering visitors a chance to see a different, more alternative side of the city. Christiania may be unconventional, but it's a part of Copenhagen's soul, reflecting the city's embrace of individuality and freedom.

1.2 History and Culture
The story of Copenhagen begins in the early Middle Ages. It is believed that the city was founded in the 10th century as a small fishing settlement. Its name, which means "merchant's harbor," speaks to its early importance as a trading hub. Located on the eastern coast of the island of Zealand, Copenhagen's position along the Øresund Strait made it an ideal location for trade and commerce, drawing merchants from all over Europe. Over time, the settlement grew in size and importance, and by the 12th century, it was declared a town by the Danish King Valdemar the Great. As the city expanded, so did its role as the political and cultural center of Denmark. In the 15th century, Copenhagen became the capital of the Danish Kingdom, a title it would retain for centuries. The city's architectural landscape began to take shape during this time, with the construction of grand buildings such as the Church of Our Lady (Vor Frue Kirke) and the fortress of Kastellet, located to the north of the city. These early structures laid the foundation for the city's future growth, with a combination of

royal palaces, churches, and public squares marking Copenhagen as a seat of power.

Throughout the 17th century, Copenhagen flourished under the reign of King Christian IV. His vision for the city transformed Copenhagen into a major European cultural center. One of his most notable contributions was the construction of Rosenborg Castle, a stunning Renaissance-style building in the city's heart. Today, Rosenborg Castle is home to the Danish crown jewels and offers visitors a glimpse into the grandeur of the Danish monarchy. Another legacy of Christian IV is the creation of the district of Christianshavn, a vibrant area now known for its modern architecture, but which in the 1600s was the heart of Copenhagen's trading activities. As Copenhagen grew in prominence, so did its cultural scene. By the 19th century, the city had become a hub for intellectuals, artists, and writers. The Danish Golden Age, a period in the early 1800s, saw the emergence of some of Denmark's greatest cultural figures. Hans Christian Andersen, perhaps the most famous of them all, wrote his beloved fairy tales while living in Copenhagen. Visitors can still trace his footsteps today, from his former residence on Nyhavn to the statue dedicated to him by the water in the city. The legacy of Andersen and the Golden Age continues to permeate the city, with theaters, museums, and art galleries celebrating Denmark's literary and artistic heritage.

Copenhagen's cultural landscape was not just shaped by Danish creators, but also by its international influences. As a thriving port city, Copenhagen attracted artists, musicians, and philosophers from across Europe. In the 19th century, the city's intellectual life was further enriched by the work of Danish philosopher Søren Kierkegaard, who explored existential themes and was based in the city throughout his life. Copenhagen's cafes and public spaces became a gathering place for these thinkers and creatives, with the vibrant energy of these discussions continuing to echo in the city's modern-day cultural venues. The 20th century brought both challenges and triumphs to Copenhagen. During World War II, Denmark was occupied by Nazi Germany, and Copenhagen, like much of the country, was thrust into a period of hardship and resistance. The city played a pivotal role in the Danish resistance movement, with many citizens risking their lives to protect Jewish families from deportation. The resilience and bravery of the Copenhagen residents during this time are still honored today, particularly in the Jewish Museum located in the heart of the city.

Post-war Copenhagen, however, saw a period of modernization and urban development. The city's commitment to design, sustainability, and innovation became evident in its expansion. The 21st century brought Copenhagen to the forefront of global cities known for their environmental consciousness. The city's ambitious plans to become carbon-neutral by 2025 reflect its commitment to sustainability, which is evident in the numerous green spaces, bike lanes, and eco-friendly buildings that dot the urban landscape. Copenhagen's cultural identity today is a blend of old-world charm and forward-thinking innovation. The city's neighborhoods are home to a vibrant mix of old and new, from the ancient, narrow streets of the Latin Quarter to the ultra-modern design hub in Vesterbro. The contrast between Copenhagen's historical buildings and cutting-edge architecture, like the Danish Architecture Center in the heart of the city, creates an energy that is both dynamic and inviting.

Visitors will find that the cultural scene in Copenhagen is as varied as its history. The city is home to an array of museums, from the renowned National Gallery of Denmark (Statens Museum for Kunst) to the experimental art spaces like the Louisiana Museum of Modern Art just outside the city. The Royal Danish Theater offers a glimpse into the city's long-standing artistic traditions, while the street art of Christiania reminds visitors of Copenhagen's progressive and alternative spirit. Copenhagen's culinary scene is another testament to the city's embrace of both tradition and innovation. The city's food culture is steeped in the legacy of Danish cuisine, with iconic dishes such as smørrebrød (open-faced sandwiches) and herring. But it is also a city of culinary experimentation, with Michelin-starred restaurants like Noma redefining the boundaries of Nordic cuisine. The food markets, such as Torvehallerne near Nørreport Station, offer a diverse range of flavors that reflect the city's multicultural influences.

1.3 Geography, Climate & Best Time to Visit
The city's landscape is shaped by its coastal location along the eastern shores of the island of Zealand, with parts of the city situated along the Øresund Strait, which separates Denmark from Sweden. With its rich history, picturesque canals, and green spaces, Copenhagen's geography not only defines its aesthetic appeal but also plays a significant role in its climate. The city's climate is influenced by its proximity to the sea, which brings mild, temperate weather, making Copenhagen a pleasant destination for visitors throughout most of the year. Understanding the city's geography and climate will help you determine the best times to visit, allowing you to make the most of your trip.

The Geography of Copenhagen
Copenhagen is located at the southernmost point of the island of Zealand, which is one of Denmark's largest islands. The city's geography is characterized by a series of interconnected waterways, canals, and green spaces, blending urban living with nature. One of Copenhagen's most notable geographical features is its waterfront, with the city hugging the shores of the Øresund Strait. The famous Nyhavn Canal is a focal point, lined with colorful buildings and bustling cafes, offering a snapshot of Copenhagen's charming maritime heritage. In addition to its waterways, Copenhagen is known for its abundance of parks and green areas, which provide a natural escape from the urban hustle. The city's layout encourages a pedestrian-friendly experience, with many attractions within walking or cycling distance of one another. The proximity to the sea also means that Copenhagen enjoys a relatively flat terrain, making it easy to explore by foot or bike. For visitors who enjoy outdoor activities, the geography of the city offers plenty of options to walk, cycle, or even kayak along its waterways and beaches.

The Climate of Copenhagen
Copenhagen experiences a temperate maritime climate, which is characterized by mild winters and cool summers. Being close to the North Sea and the Baltic Sea, the city's weather is often influenced by the surrounding waters, which moderate extreme temperature fluctuations. The climate is generally quite mild compared to other northern European cities, but it can also be unpredictable at times, with occasional rainfall and fluctuating temperatures.

Spring in Copenhagen
Spring in Copenhagen begins in March and lasts until May, marking a time of transformation as the city shakes off the chill of winter. Temperatures during this season typically range from 3°C to 12°C (37°F to 54°F), with March being the coldest month and May bringing more pleasant weather. Spring in Copenhagen is a delightful season to visit, as the city's parks and gardens begin to bloom, filling the air with the scent of fresh flowers. The famous Tivoli Gardens, for example, starts to open for the season, offering a magical experience of early blooms and quieter crowds before the summer rush. Spring is also a time when the city experiences longer daylight hours, and the parks and outdoor spaces come to life with locals and visitors enjoying outdoor cafes, walking tours, and boat rides along the canals. However, the weather can still be unpredictable, with occasional rain showers and cool winds, so packing layers and an umbrella

is essential. Despite the variability in weather, spring is considered one of the most favorable times for visitors who want to experience the city in a more relaxed atmosphere before the peak tourist season begins.

Summer in Copenhagen
Summer in Copenhagen, from June to August, is undoubtedly the most popular time to visit, and for good reason. The city enjoys its warmest temperatures during this period, ranging from 14°C to 22°C (57°F to 72°F), though temperatures can occasionally spike higher, particularly in July. This is when Copenhagen truly comes alive, with long daylight hours, outdoor festivals, and an abundance of events. The city's parks, beaches, and outdoor spaces are filled with people enjoying the sunshine, while locals and tourists alike indulge in Copenhagen's vibrant food scene, alfresco dining, and late-night strolls along the canals. Summer in Copenhagen also brings the opportunity to experience the city's rich cultural events, such as the Copenhagen Jazz Festival and the Roskilde Festival, which attract international artists and visitors. The mild temperatures and the extended daylight, with sunsets occurring as late as 10:00 p.m. in July, make it an ideal time for sightseeing and outdoor adventures. However, because summer is the peak tourist season, it's important to book accommodations and tickets to popular attractions well in advance to avoid crowds.

Autumn in Copenhagen
Autumn, from September to November, is a fantastic time to visit Copenhagen for those who prefer fewer crowds and cooler, crisp air. Temperatures during this season typically range from 9°C to 14°C (48°F to 57°F), with September still offering relatively mild weather, while November can be chilly, often dipping close to 0°C (32°F). The autumn foliage in Copenhagen's parks and gardens offers a stunning visual display, especially in areas like Frederiksberg Gardens and the King's Garden, where the trees turn rich shades of red and gold. This is also a time when the city's cultural offerings are in full swing, with theater performances, concerts, and art exhibitions taking place in various venues. The weather can be quite unpredictable, with occasional rain, so it's advisable to bring a warm jacket and prepare for changing conditions. Autumn is a wonderful time for those who prefer a quieter experience of the city, with fewer tourists and the chance to enjoy Copenhagen's cozy cafes, excellent museums, and charming streets.

Winter in Copenhagen

Winter in Copenhagen, from December to February, can be quite cold, with temperatures typically ranging from -1°C to 4°C (30°F to 39°F). Snowfall is not guaranteed, but the city does experience its fair share of chilly, grey days, often accompanied by wind and rain. Despite the cold, winter in Copenhagen has a unique charm, particularly during the Christmas season when the city transforms into a winter wonderland. The Tivoli Gardens, in particular, is a must-see during this time, as it hosts a magical Christmas market complete with twinkling lights, festive decorations, and seasonal treats. Though the weather can be harsh, winter is the perfect time for visitors who enjoy a more atmospheric, cozy experience of the city. The city's many museums, art galleries, and historical landmarks provide a warm retreat from the cold, and the holiday season brings a festive atmosphere with local markets offering Danish holiday fare and handcrafted goods. Since winter is a low season for tourism, you'll also find fewer crowds, making it easier to explore popular attractions without the long queues.

Best Time to Visit Copenhagen

The best time to visit Copenhagen depends largely on the type of experience you're seeking. Summer, with its vibrant festivals and warm weather, is ideal for those who want to experience the city at its liveliest, but it's also the most crowded and expensive time of year. If you prefer milder weather and fewer tourists, spring and autumn offer a great balance of good weather and a more peaceful atmosphere. Winter, while cold, offers a unique, festive charm and is perfect for those seeking a cozy getaway with fewer crowds and a magical holiday ambiance. Overall, Copenhagen can be visited year-round, with each season offering something unique. Whether you're cycling through the city's parks in the spring, enjoying the summer festivals, strolling through golden autumn leaves, or immersing yourself in the city's winter charm, Copenhagen has something for every traveler, no matter the season.

CHAPTER 2
ACCOMMODATION OPTIONS

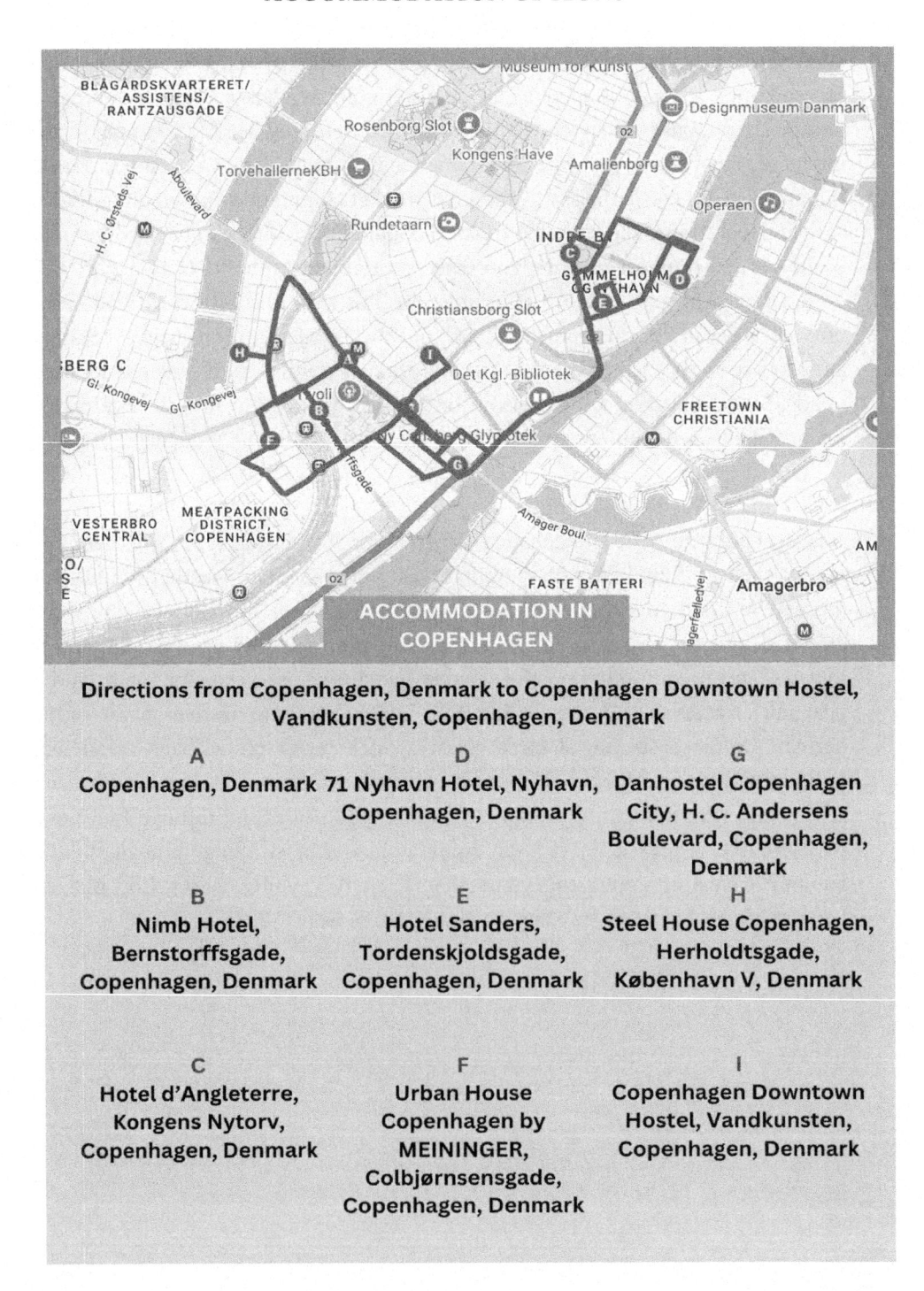

ACCOMMODATION IN COPENHAGEN

Directions from Copenhagen, Denmark to Copenhagen Downtown Hostel, Vandkunsten, Copenhagen, Denmark

A	D	G
Copenhagen, Denmark	71 Nyhavn Hotel, Nyhavn, Copenhagen, Denmark	Danhostel Copenhagen City, H. C. Andersens Boulevard, Copenhagen, Denmark
B	**E**	**H**
Nimb Hotel, Bernstorffsgade, Copenhagen, Denmark	Hotel Sanders, Tordenskjoldsgade, Copenhagen, Denmark	Steel House Copenhagen, Herholdtsgade, København V, Denmark
C	**F**	**I**
Hotel d'Angleterre, Kongens Nytorv, Copenhagen, Denmark	Urban House Copenhagen by MEININGER, Colbjørnsensgade, Copenhagen, Denmark	Copenhagen Downtown Hostel, Vandkunsten, Copenhagen, Denmark

2.1 Luxury Hotels and Boutique Hotels

Copenhagen offers a variety of accommodations that cater to every discerning traveler. From iconic, historic buildings that have been transformed into modern, elegant spaces to chic boutique properties nestled in vibrant neighborhoods, the city promises to provide a luxurious stay with exceptional service and unique offerings. Here's an exploration of distinguished hotels that stand out for their exclusivity, amenities, and the unforgettable experiences they provide.

Nimb Hotel: Located in the enchanting Tivoli Gardens, Nimb Hotel offers a truly magical experience that combines historical charm with modern luxury. This exquisite hotel occupies a prominent position within one of the world's oldest amusement parks, and its striking Moorish architecture is nothing short of breathtaking. With its 38 individually designed rooms and suites, guests can expect a blend of opulence and coziness, featuring luxurious furnishings, elegant décor, and sweeping views of Tivoli Gardens. Room rates at Nimb vary depending on the season and type of accommodation but generally range from DKK 3,000 to DKK 10,000 per night. Guests can indulge in the hotel's fine dining offerings, such as the Michelin-starred restaurant and the intimate brasserie, where meals range from DKK 200 to DKK 1,500 per person. The hotel's amenities include a private cinema, a rooftop pool, and a luxury spa. Special services like personalized concierge assistance, exclusive access to Tivoli Gardens, and curated city tours elevate the stay. For bookings and more details, visit the official website: (https://www.nimb.dk).

Hotel d'Angleterre: Hotel d'Angleterre is one of Copenhagen's most iconic luxury hotels, located in the heart of the city, just a stone's throw from Kongens Nytorv and the bustling pedestrian street, Strøget. This five-star hotel has been a symbol of luxury since 1755 and continues to offer unmatched elegance and sophistication. The hotel's 92 rooms, including 45 suites, boast a blend of classic and contemporary design, with high ceilings, ornate furnishings, and marble bathrooms. A stay at Hotel d'Angleterre is an experience in royal luxury, with prices starting around DKK 5,000 per night for a standard room, with suites costing upwards of DKK 15,000 per night. The hotel's amenities include a state-of-the-art fitness center, a lavish spa, and several exceptional dining options, including the Michelin-starred Marchal restaurant. A meal at the restaurant can cost from DKK 350 to DKK 1,800 per person, depending on the menu chosen. For those seeking personalized services, the hotel offers bespoke concierge services, private airport transfers, and customized city experiences. To book a stay, visit the official website: (https://www.dangleterre.com).

The Skt. Petri: In Copenhagen's Latin Quarter, The Skt. Petri is a sophisticated and modern boutique hotel known for its design-forward aesthetic and prime location. Located close to major attractions like the Round Tower and the National Gallery of Denmark, The Skt. Petri appeals to guests who appreciate both style and convenience. The hotel's rooms and suites are minimalistic yet stylish, with sleek modern furniture, high-end bedding, and ample natural light. Prices for a stay at The Skt. Petri typically range from DKK 2,500 to DKK 6,000 per night, depending on the room type. The hotel offers a variety of amenities, including a fitness center, an indoor pool, and a luxurious spa. The rooftop bar, with stunning views of the city, serves cocktails and light bites, while the restaurant offers a contemporary dining experience. Meals at the restaurant can range from DKK 150 to DKK 800 per person. Special services include private tour arrangements, event planning, and concierge services for guests looking for an extraordinary stay. To book a room or find more information, visit the official website: (https://www.sktpetri.com).

71 Nyhavn Hotel: For those seeking a unique blend of historic charm and contemporary luxury, 71 Nyhavn Hotel is an ideal choice. Located along the picturesque Nyhavn canal, this boutique hotel occupies two historic warehouses that date back to the 1800s. The hotel's 150 rooms and suites feature a mix of original architectural details, such as exposed beams and brick walls, along with modern amenities. Many rooms offer stunning views of the canal, offering guests a picturesque backdrop to their stay. Room rates at 71 Nyhavn typically range from DKK 2,200 to DKK 5,500 per night, with canal view rooms being among the most sought-after. Guests can enjoy dining at the hotel's restaurant, which serves contemporary Nordic cuisine with prices ranging from DKK 200 to DKK 800 per person. Additional amenities include a fitness center, bike rentals, and a business center. The hotel's concierge is available to arrange private tours, boat rides along the canal, or unique cultural experiences in Copenhagen. For more information and bookings, visit the official website: (https://www.71nyhavnhotel.dk).

Sanders: Located in the vibrant district of Frederiksstaden, Sanders is an elegant boutique hotel that combines refined design with an intimate atmosphere. This luxury property offers a personal touch, with just 54 rooms and suites, ensuring a more tailored, exclusive experience. Sanders is housed in a beautifully restored 19th-century building and features a stylish mix of Scandinavian design, modern amenities, and impeccable service. Prices for a stay at Sanders start around DKK 3,000 per night, with suites reaching upwards of DKK 7,000 per night. The hotel boasts a chic rooftop bar, a cozy lounge, and a fine dining restaurant that serves seasonal Nordic cuisine. Dining options range from DKK 150 to DKK 800 per person, and the hotel offers room service and bespoke private dining experiences for guests. Sanders also offers a range of services, including private transportation, personal shopping, and tailored concierge services to ensure a seamless experience in Copenhagen. To learn more or make a reservation, visit the official website: (https://www.sanders.dk).

2.2 Budget-Friendly Options (Hostels, Guesthouses)

Copenhagen attracts millions of visitors each year. However, despite its global appeal, the city can also be quite expensive. For travelers seeking affordable yet comfortable accommodation, there are several budget-friendly options, including hostels and guesthouses, that provide the perfect base for exploring the city. These accommodations offer a blend of convenience, value for money, and local charm, ensuring that visitors can enjoy Copenhagen without breaking the bank.

Urban House Copenhagen by MEININGER
Located in the heart of Vesterbro, one of Copenhagen's most trendy and lively districts, Urban House Copenhagen by MEININGER offers a stylish and modern environment for budget-conscious travelers. This hostel is just a short walk from the bustling Tivoli Gardens, the central train station, and the iconic Stroget shopping street, making it an ideal choice for those looking to be close to Copenhagen's top attractions. Prices at Urban House start around DKK 200 per night for a dormitory bed, with private rooms starting at DKK 800. The hostel is known for its cool, urban atmosphere and a variety of modern amenities. Guests can enjoy free Wi-Fi, a fully equipped guest kitchen, and a vibrant common area perfect for socializing or relaxing. The hostel also features a bar where guests can unwind after a day of sightseeing. Urban House offers bike rentals, providing an easy and eco-friendly way to explore the city like a local. The hostel's staff is particularly helpful and can assist with booking tickets for attractions and providing insider tips on Copenhagen's best-kept secrets. For meals, guests can opt for reasonably priced breakfast options or prepare their own food in the kitchen. The neighborhood offers many affordable dining spots

as well. To make a reservation and for more details, visit their official website at (https://shorturl.at/0pHIB).

Danhostel Copenhagen City
Another excellent budget option is Danhostel Copenhagen City, one of the largest and most popular hostels in Denmark. Situated along the scenic harbor, just a few minutes' walk from the central station and major attractions like the National Museum and Christiansborg Palace, this hostel offers an excellent central location. Prices for a bed in a shared dormitory begin at DKK 200 per night, while private rooms are available from around DKK 650. Danhostel Copenhagen City offers a variety of amenities to enhance guests' stay, including a restaurant serving breakfast, lunch, and dinner with a focus on Danish cuisine. Guests can also access free Wi-Fi throughout the property, a large communal kitchen for cooking their own meals, and a lounge area with a panoramic view of the city. The hostel also provides bike rentals, a great way to navigate Copenhagen's many cycling paths. The spacious and modern design of the hostel, combined with its vibrant atmosphere, makes it an excellent choice for travelers of all ages. Danhostel also has a range of special services, such as group booking facilities for those traveling with larger parties and a 24-hour reception for added convenience. For more information and to book a stay, visit their official website at (https://www.danhostelcopenhagen.dk).

The Sleep Boutique Hostel
The Sleep Boutique Hostel is located in the city center, within walking distance of Copenhagen Central Station and the famous Tivoli Gardens. This small and intimate hostel focuses on providing a cozy and comfortable atmosphere for travelers. With beds in dormitories starting at DKK 250 per night and private rooms from DKK 900, The Sleep Boutique Hostel is an affordable option that does not compromise on comfort or quality. This hostel is unique in that it blends a boutique-style interior with a hostel setup, offering a more personalized and peaceful environment than many larger hostels. Amenities include free Wi-Fi, a fully equipped kitchen, and a small café where guests can enjoy coffee and light snacks. The hostel is known for its friendly and welcoming staff, who go out of their way to make guests feel at home. For those looking to enjoy Copenhagen on a budget, The Sleep Boutique Hostel also offers discounts on local attractions and tours. Additionally, the hostel provides guests with access to a lounge area, a book exchange corner, and free luggage storage. The neighborhood around the hostel is known for its local eateries, which offer

delicious Danish dishes at affordable prices. For more information and to make a reservation, visit their official website at (https://www.sleepboutique.dk).

Steel House Copenhagen
For those seeking a more modern and upscale hostel experience, Steel House Copenhagen is a top choice. Located in the vibrant Vesterbro district, close to the city center and major attractions, this hostel combines industrial design with comfort and style. Prices for dormitory beds start at DKK 250 per night, while private rooms begin at DKK 850, making it an attractive choice for those willing to spend a little more for a more premium hostel experience. Steel House offers a range of high-end amenities, including an indoor swimming pool, a gym, and a sauna—rare features in most hostels. Guests can enjoy a spacious common area with a bar and restaurant serving light meals and drinks. The hostel also offers a fully equipped kitchen for guests who prefer to cook their own meals. Wi-Fi is free throughout the building, and the reception offers 24-hour service. Steel House Copenhagen is also known for its commitment to sustainability, with eco-friendly practices incorporated throughout the hostel. With its sleek design, excellent location, and modern amenities, Steel House offers a stylish and affordable place to stay for travelers who enjoy contemporary design and a relaxed atmosphere. To book your stay and find more information, visit their official website at (https://www.steelhouse.dk).

The Little Guesthouse
For a more intimate and homely experience, The Little Guesthouse is a charming and budget-friendly guesthouse located in the Frederiksberg area, which is known for its leafy streets and tranquil ambiance. Just a short metro ride from the city center, this guesthouse offers rooms starting at DKK 450 per night. The Little Guesthouse prides itself on providing a warm, welcoming environment for travelers. The rooms are simply but tastefully furnished, with a focus on comfort and relaxation. Guests can enjoy a shared kitchen, where they can prepare their meals, and a cozy lounge area to unwind after a day of sightseeing. The guesthouse also offers free Wi-Fi, tea and coffee facilities, and the option to rent bikes for exploring Copenhagen's scenic neighborhoods. While the guesthouse does not have a restaurant, there are numerous local cafés and eateries within walking distance, offering delicious and affordable Danish fare. What sets The Little Guesthouse apart is its personal touch, as the owners take the time to interact with guests and share insider tips about Copenhagen. This makes it a fantastic choice for those looking for a more local experience

during their stay. For more details and bookings, visit their official website at (https://www.littleguesthouse.dk).

2.3 Vacation Rentals and Apartments

Copenhagen provides a range of lodging experiences that promise both comfort and convenience. For those seeking a more personalized, home-like stay, vacation rentals and apartments are a perfect choice. These accommodations offer the flexibility of self-catering, private spaces, and an authentic taste of Danish living. Below, we explore unique vacation rentals and apartments in Copenhagen, each with its own distinctive appeal, prime location, and services that will make your stay both enjoyable and memorable.

The Apartments at Kongens Nytorv: Situated in the heart of Copenhagen, The Apartments at Kongens Nytorv offers a perfect blend of modern amenities and historical surroundings. Located just steps away from some of Copenhagen's most iconic attractions, such as Nyhavn, the Royal Danish Theatre, and Amalienborg Palace, this rental provides guests with easy access to the city's vibrant culture. These contemporary apartments are spacious, beautifully designed, and equipped with all the essentials for a comfortable stay. Guests can expect full kitchens, living areas with flat-screen TVs, and free Wi-Fi throughout the property. Prices for a one-bedroom apartment start at approximately DKK 1,500 per night, with larger apartments for families or groups available at higher rates. Guests will enjoy a modern, stylish interior with sleek Scandinavian design elements. The building also offers concierge services, ensuring that all your needs are taken care of. In terms of dining, guests can prepare their own meals in fully equipped kitchens, or explore the numerous cafes and restaurants nearby. Breakfast options are available for a small additional charge, and the nearby area offers a variety of meal choices, from traditional Danish smørrebrød to international cuisine. For more information and to book a stay, visit the official website (https://www.apartmentskongensnytorv.com).

Copenhagen Downtown Hostel: Located in the vibrant downtown area, Copenhagen Downtown Hostel offers budget-friendly vacation rentals for those who want to experience the city without breaking the bank. Situated in a charming building, this hostel is not only known for its affordability but also its excellent atmosphere and design. The rooms and dormitories are spacious, clean, and decorated in a simple yet stylish Scandinavian design, making it an ideal base for those who prefer a more social and communal style of lodging. Prices for dormitory beds start at DKK 200 per night, while private rooms range from DKK 600 to DKK 1,200 per night, depending on the season and room size. The hostel also provides shared kitchen facilities where guests can prepare their own meals, and an on-site bar that offers a great selection of drinks and light bites. The unique feature of this accommodation is its social atmosphere, with regular events and activities organized for guests to meet and interact. For more details or to reserve your stay, check their website (https://www.cphdowntownhostel.com).

Lovely Studio Apartments in Vesterbro: For travelers seeking a more intimate and residential experience, Lovely Studio Apartments in Vesterbro offers an ideal retreat. Located in one of Copenhagen's most vibrant and trendy neighborhoods, Vesterbro, these apartments provide a comfortable, private space for individuals or couples. Vesterbro is known for its artistic flair, diverse dining scene, and vibrant nightlife, making it a perfect choice for those who want to experience the local lifestyle. The apartments are compact yet well-designed, with a focus on functionality and comfort. Each unit features a fully equipped kitchen, a cozy living space, and modern amenities such as free Wi-Fi, a flat-screen TV, and air conditioning. Prices for a studio apartment range from DKK 900 to DKK 1,400 per night, depending on the season and length of stay. Guests can enjoy breakfast at nearby cafes or prepare their own meals in the apartment. Special services include daily cleaning, and the host can provide insider tips on the best local restaurants and events. Visit their official website (https://www.lovelystudioapartment.dk) to make a reservation or to learn more.

Urban Living in the Heart of Christianshavn: If you're looking for a unique and luxurious experience, Urban Living in Christianshavn offers stunning apartments right along the canals of Copenhagen. This upscale neighborhood is known for its modern architecture, fine dining restaurants, and vibrant cultural scene. The apartments themselves boast floor-to-ceiling windows that offer spectacular views of the water and the city skyline. Each unit is fully furnished with designer furniture, premium kitchen appliances, and luxurious amenities, ensuring a five-star experience. Prices for these luxurious apartments start at DKK 2,000 per night, with larger suites and penthouses available for higher rates. The apartments come with all the expected modern conveniences, including a high-end kitchen, spacious living area, free Wi-Fi, and access to private balconies. Guests can also enjoy additional services, such as grocery delivery, private chef experiences, and on-demand concierge assistance. Dining options in the area are abundant, with some of Copenhagen's best restaurants just a short walk away. For more information and booking, visit their official website (https://www.urbanlivingchristianshavn.dk).

The Green Door Apartments: For those seeking a peaceful and serene atmosphere without being too far from the city's attractions, The Green Door Apartments offer a perfect escape. Located in the quiet neighborhood of Frederiksberg, just a short distance from Copenhagen's city center, these apartments are surrounded by green spaces, tranquil parks, and local cafes. The apartments are designed with an emphasis on nature, featuring earthy tones, natural wood, and plenty of plants, creating a peaceful retreat from the hustle and bustle of the city. Prices for a one-bedroom apartment at The Green Door Apartments begin at DKK 1,000 per night. The apartments include a fully equipped kitchen, living area, and modern amenities such as free Wi-Fi and a flat-screen TV. Guests can enjoy the serenity of the private garden, where they can relax and unwind after a day of sightseeing. Special services include bicycle rentals for exploring the city, as well as an organic breakfast option delivered to your door. For more information and reservations, visit their official website (https://www.thegreendoorapartments.dk).

2.4 Unique Stays: Historic Buildings and Design Hotels

Copenhagen boasts a rich variety of accommodations, especially for travelers seeking something more unique and memorable than the conventional hotel experience. Historic buildings, design hotels, and charming boutique stays offer visitors an opportunity to immerse themselves in the city's aesthetic history and contemporary flair. In this guide, we explore five exceptional stays that will not only provide comfort but also immerse guests in the very essence of Copenhagen's cultural and design scene. Each of these accommodations stands out for its distinctive architecture, historic charm, and unparalleled hospitality, making them perfect choices for anyone looking to experience the city's creative spirit.

Hotel d'Angleterre: One of Copenhagen's most iconic hotels, Hotel d'Angleterre is a luxurious property located in the heart of the city, at Kongens Nytorv square. Established in 1755, this historic hotel has been a landmark in Copenhagen for centuries and remains a symbol of elegance and refinement. The grand façade and ornate interiors reflect the hotel's storied past, yet modern renovations have ensured that it meets the highest standards of contemporary luxury. The hotel features beautifully appointed rooms, with rich fabrics, antique furniture, and magnificent chandeliers. For those looking for something truly special, the Royal Suite offers unmatched luxury with its panoramic views over the city. Prices for a standard room start at approximately DKK 3,500 per night, while suites like the Royal Suite can cost upwards of DKK 50,000 per night. Amenities include a world-class spa, an indoor pool, and a renowned fitness center, offering guests the utmost in relaxation and rejuvenation. Dining options are plentiful, with the Michelin-starred restaurant "Marchal" providing an exquisite menu focusing on French cuisine paired with the finest wines. A meal at Marchal can cost around DKK 700-1,200 per person for a three-course dinner. For bookings, visit the official website at (https://www.dangleterre.com).

Nimb Hotel: Nimb Hotel is a historic hotel that combines fairy-tale romance with modern luxury. The hotel's design is an enchanting blend of Moorish architecture and whimsical features, making it one of the most visually stunning properties in Copenhagen. Nimb's location inside Tivoli Gardens means that guests are surrounded by the charm and beauty of one of the world's oldest amusement parks, creating an experience unlike any other. The rooms and suites at Nimb are opulent, featuring ornate wooden beams, plush furnishings, and high ceilings. Many of the rooms offer views of Tivoli Gardens, providing a front-row seat to the park's vibrant colors and lively atmosphere. Prices for a standard room begin at approximately DKK 3,200 per night, with suites starting around DKK 6,500. The hotel also offers a range of exclusive services such as private park access, guided tours of Tivoli, and a personal concierge to help guests plan their stay. Dining at Nimb is an experience in itself, with several restaurants on the premises. The Michelin-starred "Nimb Brasserie" offers a delicious menu of French-inspired dishes, with prices for a three-course meal starting at DKK 700. To reserve a stay, visit Nimb Hotel's official website at (https://www.nimb.dk/en).

71 Nyhavn Hotel: For those who want to experience Copenhagen's vibrant harbor life, 71 Nyhavn Hotel offers a perfect blend of historic charm and modern amenities. Set in a converted warehouse dating back to the early 19th century, the hotel is located along the picturesque Nyhavn canal, with stunning views of the colorful buildings lining the waterfront. Its location places guests in the heart of Copenhagen's bustling cultural district, just steps away from top restaurants, museums, and historic landmarks. The hotel's design preserves much of the original architecture, such as wooden beams and brick walls, while incorporating modern touches for comfort. Rooms are elegantly furnished with a mix of classic and contemporary décor. Rates for a standard room begin at around DKK 2,000 per night, with larger rooms and suites available for a premium. 71 Nyhavn Hotel also offers exclusive services like private boat tours along the canal, ensuring guests enjoy the scenic beauty of Copenhagen from a unique perspective. For dining, the hotel's restaurant offers a menu focused on Scandinavian cuisine, with prices for a meal ranging from DKK 250-600 per person. To book a stay, visit (https://www.71nyhavn.dk).

Axel Guldsmeden: Axel Guldsmeden is one of Copenhagen's most stylish design hotels, combining a chic boutique experience with a commitment to sustainability. Situated in the vibrant Vesterbro district, the hotel is housed in a beautifully restored historic building, and its interiors are a perfect blend of Scandinavian minimalism and bohemian charm. Axel Guldsmeden is especially popular among eco-conscious travelers, thanks to its environmentally friendly practices, including organic food offerings, eco-friendly toiletries, and sustainable design elements. Rooms are cozy yet stylish, decorated with bamboo floors, large beds, and vintage furnishings. A standard room starts at around DKK 1,200 per night, with more luxurious rooms available for higher rates. The hotel's amenities include a wellness center with a sauna, a rooftop garden, and a charming café serving organic coffee and light meals. Guests can enjoy a meal at the hotel's restaurant, which serves an organic, farm-to-table menu with prices for a three-course meal starting at DKK 500. For bookings and more details, visit Axel Guldsmeden's website at (https://www.guldsmedenhotels.com/axel).

SP34: For those who wish to be at the center of Copenhagen's thriving design and creative scene, SP34 is an ideal choice. Located in the Latin Quarter, just a short walk from the city's top attractions, SP34 is a boutique hotel that beautifully balances modern design with the city's historical charm. The hotel occupies a former townhouse, with carefully curated interiors that reflect Copenhagen's iconic style, from the minimalist furniture to the clean lines and elegant finishes. SP34's rooms offer a relaxing, contemporary atmosphere, with an emphasis on comfort and style. A standard room starts at approximately DKK 1,500 per night, with suites available for more. The hotel offers a variety of services, including a popular wine bar, a trendy restaurant focusing on Nordic cuisine, and a fitness center. The restaurant is known for its locally sourced, seasonal ingredients, with prices for a meal starting at DKK 350 per person. To learn more or make a reservation, visit SP34's official website at (https://www.sphotel.dk).

2.5 Local Neighborhoods and Areas to Stay

Copenhagen has something for every traveler. Exploring different neighborhoods is one of the best ways to experience the city, as each offers its own unique ambiance, charm, and range of accommodation options. From chic boutique hotels in fashionable districts to charming guesthouses in quieter areas, here's a guide to the best neighborhoods to stay in Copenhagen.

Nyhavn: Nyhavn, perhaps the most iconic district in Copenhagen, is known for its colorful 17th-century townhouses lining the vibrant canal. This picturesque neighborhood offers a truly unique setting, with a mix of traditional Danish architecture and modern restaurants, cafes, and boutiques. The area is situated at the heart of the city, making it an ideal base for exploring Copenhagen's many cultural landmarks, such as the Royal Danish Playhouse and Amalienborg Palace. Accommodation options in Nyhavn range from boutique hotels to high-end apartments overlooking the water. Prices for lodging typically start around DKK 1,800 per night for a standard room in a 3-star hotel, with upscale accommodations in luxury hotels or apartments with canal views reaching DKK 5,000 and beyond. The area is home to some excellent dining spots, with meals ranging from DKK 150 for a casual bite to DKK 800 for a fine-dining experience. Unique features of this neighborhood include its vibrant atmosphere, the ability to enjoy canal tours right from the harbor, and easy access to Copenhagen's shopping district. For more details and bookings, visit (https://www.71nyhavnhotel.dk).

Vesterbro: Vesterbro is one of Copenhagen's most vibrant and up-and-coming neighborhoods, known for its trendy atmosphere and artistic flair. Once an industrial area, it has undergone a transformation into a dynamic hub filled with cafes, bars, galleries, and boutique shops. Located just a short distance from the Central Station, Vesterbro is an ideal area for those looking for a lively and youthful environment. It is also home to the popular Meatpacking District, where visitors can experience Copenhagen's nightlife scene. Staying in Vesterbro means immersing yourself in the creative energy of the district. The area offers a range of accommodations, from hip hostels to chic boutique hotels. Lodging prices generally range from DKK 1,200 per night in budget accommodations to DKK 4,000 for more luxurious hotel rooms. The amenities in this district include trendy cafés, local eateries serving modern Nordic cuisine, and excellent public transport connections. Meals here are typically affordable, ranging from DKK 100 for a casual meal to DKK 600 for a gourmet dining experience. Visitors to Vesterbro will also enjoy its proximity to the famous Tivoli Gardens and the Copenhagen Central Station, making it easy to explore the rest of the city. For booking and more details, visit (https://www.hotelottilia.com).

Frederiksberg: Frederiksberg is a beautiful, residential neighborhood that offers a peaceful escape from the hustle and bustle of central Copenhagen. Known for its wide boulevards, tree-lined streets, and stately architecture, Frederiksberg is one of the most affluent areas in the city. It's also home to Frederiksberg Gardens, one of Copenhagen's most scenic parks, and the Copenhagen Zoo, making it an excellent location for families and nature lovers. Accommodation in Frederiksberg is varied, with elegant hotels offering a more relaxed, upscale experience compared to the city center. Prices typically range from DKK 1,500 for more affordable hotels to DKK 4,500 for luxury accommodations. The area is known for its calm, family-friendly atmosphere, perfect for visitors who enjoy a more serene stay, yet still want to be close to the city's main attractions. The district also boasts a number of fine dining options, with prices ranging from DKK 200 for a casual meal to DKK 1,200 for an exquisite gourmet experience. Visitors can easily explore the neighborhood's lush green spaces and walk to nearby shopping streets. For more information and bookings, visit (https://www.scandichotels.com/falkoner).

Nørrebro: Nørrebro is one of Copenhagen's most diverse and eclectic neighborhoods, known for its multicultural vibe and an abundance of independent shops, global cuisine, and alternative culture. This lively district is home to many students, artists, and young professionals, creating an atmosphere full of creativity and energy. With its mix of trendy bars, vintage shops, and bustling markets, Nørrebro offers an authentic slice of local life. Accommodations in Nørrebro tend to be more budget-friendly compared to other central districts, though there are still some great boutique hotels and guesthouses. Prices for lodging generally range from DKK 1,000 for a budget room in a guesthouse to DKK 3,000 for a boutique hotel room. The neighborhood is known for its vibrant food scene, offering everything from street food stalls to high-end dining establishments. Meals in Nørrebro typically cost between DKK 100 to DKK 500. Special services and unique features of the area include a close-knit community, the lively Sankt Hans Torv square, and a wide variety of cultural events and festivals. For bookings and more information, visit (https://www.avenuehotel.dk).

Christianshavn: Christianshavn is one of Copenhagen's most sought-after neighborhoods, known for its upscale waterfront properties and trendy atmosphere. Located along the city's harbor, this area has undergone significant redevelopment in recent years and is now home to a thriving dining scene, high-end residences, and cultural landmarks such as the famous Opera House and the cutting-edge Design Museum Denmark. It is also close to the popular Freetown Christiania, a quirky, self-proclaimed autonomous district that draws visitors with its unique alternative lifestyle. Accommodation in Christianshavn offers a mix of contemporary luxury hotels and chic boutique options. Lodging prices range from DKK 2,500 per night for a standard room to DKK 6,000 for more exclusive waterfront suites. The neighborhood is home to several world-renowned restaurants, with meal prices ranging from DKK 150 for casual dining to DKK 1,500 for a multi-course fine dining experience. With its proximity to the water, many of the hotels in Christianshavn offer stunning views and relaxing atmospheres. Guests can also enjoy easy access to walking paths along the harbor and boat tours around the city. For more details and bookings, visit (https://www.admiralhotel.dk).

CHAPTER 3
TRANSPORTATION

3.1 Getting to Copenhagen

Copenhagen is a city that seamlessly blends historic charm with modern vibrancy. Known for its picturesque canals, vibrant neighborhoods, and the iconic Little Mermaid statue, the city welcomes millions of visitors each year. Whether you're arriving by air, train, or road, the journey to Copenhagen is as delightful as the destination itself. Here's an extensive guide to help you plan your travels to this Scandinavian jewel.

Arriving in Copenhagen by Air Travel

For most international visitors, arriving in Copenhagen by air is the most convenient option. Copenhagen Airport, known as Kastrup (CPH), is Denmark's largest airport and one of the busiest in Northern Europe. Situated just 8 kilometers south of the city center, it serves as a major gateway to the region, offering excellent connectivity to cities across Europe, North America, Asia, and beyond. Numerous airlines operate flights to Copenhagen, catering to a wide range of budgets. Scandinavian Airlines (SAS) is the flag carrier of Denmark and offers direct flights from major hubs such as New York, London, and Paris. For budget travelers, carriers like Ryanair (https://www.ryanair.com)), Norwegian Air (https://www.norwegian.com)), and easyJet (https://www.easyjet.com) provide economical options from European cities. Traditional airlines such as British Airways (https://www.britishairways.com) and Lufthansa (https://www.lufthansa.com) also serve Copenhagen with frequent connections. Ticket prices vary depending on the time of booking, travel season, and departure location. On average, round-trip flights from major European cities range between €100-€300, while intercontinental flights can cost between €500-€1,200. Booking well in advance typically secures the best deals. Popular platforms like Skyscanner (https://www.skyscanner.net) and Expedia (https://www.expedia.com) allow travelers to compare prices, while airline websites often feature exclusive discounts. Copenhagen Airport is highly efficient, featuring modern facilities such as free Wi-Fi, dining options, and shopping. The Copenhagen Metro (https://www.m.dk) connects the airport to the city center in just 15 minutes. Alternatively, visitors can opt for taxis or Movia Buses (https://www.moviatrafik.dk) for a more leisurely transfer.

Reaching Copenhagen by Train

Traveling to Copenhagen by train offers a scenic and relaxing experience, particularly for visitors exploring Europe. Copenhagen is a major rail hub, and its central station, Københavns Hovedbanegård, is well-connected to cities across Denmark and neighboring countries. International travelers can enjoy direct train services from cities like Hamburg, Berlin, and Stockholm. Deutsche Bahn (https://www.bahn.com) operates regular services from Germany, including the EuroCity train, which crosses the awe-inspiring Øresund Bridge connecting Sweden to Denmark. Visitors from Sweden can also rely on SJ Trains (https://www.sj.se), which provide swift connections from Malmö, Gothenburg, and Stockholm. Ticket prices depend on the route and booking date. A one-way ticket from Hamburg to Copenhagen typically costs between €40-€100. To secure affordable rates, book early via Danish State Railways (DSB) (https://www.dsb.dk), Trainline (https://www.thetrainline.com), or the respective international rail services.

Exploring Road Travel to Copenhagen

For those who enjoy the freedom of road trips, driving or taking a bus to Copenhagen offers a unique and flexible way to explore the region. The city is well-connected by an extensive network of highways, making it easily accessible from neighboring countries like Germany and Sweden. Visitors driving from Germany can take the E45 highway leading directly to Denmark, while the iconic Øresund Bridge offers a direct link from Sweden. Drivers crossing the bridge should anticipate a toll fee, approximately €50 for a standard car, which can be paid online via the Øresund Bridge website (https://www.oresundsbron.com). For those without a car, long-distance bus services offer a budget-friendly alternative. FlixBus (https://www.flixbus.com) and Eurolines (https://www.eurolines.eu) operate regular routes to Copenhagen from major European cities. Tickets often start as low as €20 for shorter routes, and bookings can be made directly through their websites. These buses are equipped with modern amenities, including Wi-Fi, power outlets, and comfortable seats, ensuring a pleasant journey. Road travel allows for leisurely exploration of quaint towns and stunning landscapes along the way. Rest stops and scenic viewpoints provide opportunities to relax and absorb the beauty of the Nordic region, making the drive to Copenhagen an adventure in itself.

Essential Tips for a Smooth Journey

No matter how you choose to arrive in Copenhagen, thorough preparation ensures a seamless trip. Denmark uses the Danish Krone (DKK), so it's wise to have local currency on hand for immediate expenses like public transportation or refreshments. Fortunately, credit cards are widely accepted, and ATMs are readily available. If you're traveling by train or bus, consider downloading travel apps such as Trainline or FlixBus to keep track of your bookings and receive updates. For air travelers, the Copenhagen Airport app (https://www.cph.dk) offers helpful insights on flight statuses and airport navigation.

3.2 Public Transportation Options (Metro, Bus, Train)

Copenhagen seamlessly combines efficiency, sustainability, and accessibility. Whether you are visiting for a few days or an extended period, the city offers a variety of transport modes, including metro, buses, and trains, to ensure that every corner of Copenhagen and its surrounding areas is within reach. For visitors, understanding how to navigate these options and their pricing will transform your experience into one of convenience and comfort.

The Metro: Copenhagen's metro system is often hailed as one of the best in the world. Fully automated and operating 24 hours a day, the metro is the backbone of public transport in the city. With four lines—M1, M2, M3 (Cityringen), and M4—the metro covers key areas, including the city center, the airport, and neighborhoods such as Frederiksberg, Nørrebro, and Østerbro. The metro is an excellent choice for visitors arriving at Copenhagen Airport, as it connects directly to the city center in just 15 minutes. Trains arrive every few minutes, ensuring minimal waiting time. Stations are equipped with clear signage in both Danish and English, making it easy for first-time visitors to navigate. Tickets for the metro are part of the integrated Copenhagen public transport system, which uses a zone-based fare system. A single journey ticket costs around DKK 24-36, depending on the number of zones traveled. For tourists, the Copenhagen Card or a City Pass offers unlimited travel across all public transportation modes within selected zones, making it a cost-effective choice. Tickets can be purchased at station kiosks, ticket machines, or through the DOT app, which is available in English and user-friendly. For more information, visit the official metro website at (https://www.m.dk/).

Buses: Copenhagen's bus network complements the metro system by reaching areas that are not directly accessible by train. The city operates regular buses, night buses, and harbor buses, catering to both locals and visitors at all times of the day. The iconic yellow city buses serve numerous routes across Copenhagen, stopping frequently and connecting the city's attractions, neighborhoods, and suburbs. Visitors looking to explore cultural landmarks like the Little Mermaid statue or the Nyhavn harbor can easily hop on one of these buses. Night buses ensure safe and reliable transportation after the metro has reduced its frequency late at night. For a unique experience, the harbor buses traverse the city's waterways, offering scenic views of the harbor while connecting key points such as Nyhavn, the Opera House, and the Royal Library. Harbor buses are included in the same ticketing system as other modes of public transport. Ticket prices for buses are aligned with the metro and train systems, with single tickets starting at DKK 24-36. Payment can be made using the DOT app, or passengers can use the Copenhagen Card for unlimited travel. More information on bus schedules and routes can be found at (https://www.dinoffentligetransport.dk/).

Trains: Trains play a vital role in connecting Copenhagen with its suburbs, neighboring towns, and even countries. The S-Tog system, identified by its red trains, is a suburban rail network that covers Greater Copenhagen. With seven lines and frequent departures, the S-Tog is ideal for day trips to attractions outside the city center, such as Dyrehaven park or the charming town of Hillerød, home to Frederiksborg Castle. For travelers wishing to venture further, the regional trains link Copenhagen to cities like Roskilde and Helsingør, where you can visit the Viking Ship Museum or Kronborg Castle, respectively. These trains also connect Denmark's capital to Malmö, Sweden, via the iconic Øresund Bridge. Train fares are zone-based and align with the metro and bus ticketing system. A single journey within the city typically costs DKK 24-36, while regional trips to destinations like Roskilde are priced at approximately DKK 96. Tickets can be purchased at stations or through the DOT app. For train schedules and additional details, visit (https://www.dsb.dk/).

Integrated Ticketing and Apps for Easy Navigation
One of the most convenient features of Copenhagen's public transportation system is its integrated ticketing system, which covers the metro, buses, and trains. This means a single ticket or pass can be used across all modes of transport within the designated zones. For tourists, the Copenhagen Card is highly recommended. Available for 24, 48, 72, 96, or 120 hours, this card not

only provides unlimited access to public transportation but also includes free entry to over 80 attractions. Prices start at DKK 419 for a 24-hour card, making it an excellent value for travelers eager to explore the city. The card can be purchased at the airport or online at (https://www.copenhagencard.com/). Alternatively, the City Pass is another budget-friendly option for unlimited travel within selected zones. Both cards can be purchased online or at the airport upon arrival. The DOT app is an indispensable tool for navigating Copenhagen's transport network. It allows users to plan routes, check schedules, and purchase tickets seamlessly. Available in English, the app ensures that visitors can confidently travel without the stress of language barriers. For more details, visit the app's website at (https://www.dinoffentligetransport.dk/).

Practical Tips for Public Transportation in Copenhagen
Travelers new to Copenhagen will find the public transportation system straightforward and accommodating. Stations and vehicles are equipped with clear signage, and announcements are often made in English. Maps and guides are readily available at stations, and the helpful staff are usually fluent in English and willing to assist. Accessibility is a priority in Copenhagen, with elevators and ramps available at most metro and train stations, as well as low-floor buses to accommodate wheelchairs and strollers. Peak hours can be busy, particularly on weekdays, so visitors are advised to plan their journeys accordingly to avoid crowds. Remember to validate your ticket before boarding, as fines for traveling without a valid ticket can be steep.

3.3 Taxi and Ride-Hailing Services

Copenhagen offers a variety of transportation options that make navigating the city both efficient and comfortable. For those seeking the convenience of door-to-door service, taxi and ride-hailing services provide a reliable and accessible solution. Whether traveling for business, leisure, or a blend of both, understanding these services ensures visitors can move around the city with ease and confidence.

Traditional Taxis: Taxis in Copenhagen are widely available and provide a dependable way to travel. Whether hailing a cab on the street, booking through a phone call, or finding one at designated taxi stands near major attractions, hotels, and the airport, the process is straightforward and hassle-free. Taxi services are regulated in Denmark, ensuring high standards of professionalism, safety, and transparency. The cost of a taxi ride in Copenhagen includes a base fare of approximately DKK 40 to DKK 50, with an additional DKK 15 to DKK 20 per kilometer. Night rates and weekend surcharges may apply, increasing the total fare slightly. A typical trip from Copenhagen Airport to the city center costs around DKK 250 to DKK 400, depending on traffic conditions. Copenhagen's taxis are modern, often equipped with card payment options, free Wi-Fi, and spacious interiors to accommodate travelers with luggage. Drivers are fluent in English, making communication seamless for international visitors. For reliable taxi services, you can visit the following websites: TAXA 4x35: (http://www.taxa.dk), Dantaxi: (http://www.dantaxi.dk).

Ride-Hailing Services: Ride-hailing services offer a tech-savvy and often cost-effective alternative to traditional taxis. Companies like Bolt and Uber operate in Copenhagen, catering to travelers who prefer the convenience of booking a ride via a smartphone app. These platforms provide features such as upfront pricing, estimated arrival times, and real-time ride tracking, making them particularly appealing to visitors unfamiliar with the city. Prices for ride-hailing services are generally competitive, with fares for short rides starting around DKK 50 to DKK 75. Trips from the airport to central Copenhagen typically range between DKK 200 and DKK 350, depending on the type of vehicle chosen and the time of day. Ride-hailing apps also allow users to select from various vehicle categories, from standard cars to premium options, ensuring a tailored experience. For more information and to book rides, visitors can use the following services: Bolt: (https://www.bolt.eu), Uber: (https://www.uber.com).

Luxury and Specialized Taxi Services
For travelers seeking an elevated experience, Copenhagen offers a selection of luxury taxi services. Companies like Blacklane and Dantaxi provide high-end vehicles, including sedans and SUVs, with professional drivers trained to offer exceptional service. These services are ideal for business travelers, special occasions, or those simply wanting to indulge in a touch of luxury. Luxury taxi fares start at approximately DKK 400 and can exceed DKK 1,000 for longer journeys or premium vehicles. Bookings for these services can be made online or through dedicated apps, often with the option to include amenities like Wi-Fi, refreshments, and luggage assistance. Additionally, Copenhagen features eco-friendly taxi options, such as hybrid or electric vehicles, catering to environmentally conscious travelers. These services are typically priced similarly to standard taxis, offering a sustainable yet convenient way to explore

the city. For luxury or eco-friendly taxi options, you can check out: Blacklane: (https://www.blacklane.com), Dantaxi (Eco-Friendly Option): (http://www.dantaxi.dk).

Navigating Copenhagen with Taxis and Ride-Hailing Services
Visitors to Copenhagen can navigate the city's taxi and ride-hailing services effectively by following a few key tips. For traditional taxis, it is recommended to use official taxi stands or pre-book rides through reputable companies such as TAXA 4x35 or Dantaxi. This ensures a secure and reliable experience while avoiding unlicensed operators. Ride-hailing apps like Bolt and Uber can be downloaded and used directly from a smartphone, with most platforms supporting international payment methods, including major credit cards and digital wallets. It's advisable to check the app's fare estimate and availability in advance, particularly during peak hours or large events when demand may be high.To save on costs, consider sharing rides through carpooling features available in some ride-hailing apps. These services allow multiple passengers heading in similar directions to share a single vehicle, reducing both expenses and environmental impact.

Accessibility and Inclusivity
Copenhagen's taxi and ride-hailing services prioritize accessibility, offering options for travelers with specific needs. Wheelchair-accessible taxis can be booked through specialized providers, and most drivers are trained to assist passengers with mobility challenges. Families traveling with young children can request vehicles equipped with child safety seats, ensuring a safe and comfortable journey for all. For those traveling in groups, larger vehicles such as minivans are readily available through both taxi companies and ride-hailing platforms. These vehicles provide ample space for passengers and luggage, making them ideal for group outings or airport transfers.

3.4 Cycling and Bike-Friendly Infrastructure

Copenhagen stands as one of the world's most bike-friendly cities, and its commitment to cycling infrastructure makes it a model for other urban areas striving to promote sustainability and healthy living. With an extensive network of bike lanes, bike-sharing schemes, and supportive policies, the city provides an ideal environment for cyclists of all levels. Whether you're a casual tourist or an experienced cyclist, navigating Copenhagen by bike is not only practical but also a deeply rewarding experience. This guide will provide an in-depth look at the various cycling infrastructures available in Copenhagen, how to navigate them, and the pricing systems in place.

The Cycling Network in Copenhagen: Copenhagen's cycling network is renowned for its comprehensive coverage and user-friendliness. The city's commitment to cycling is reflected in the fact that approximately 40% of Copenhageners commute by bike daily. The city boasts over 390 kilometers of dedicated cycling lanes, making it one of the most cycle-friendly metropolises globally. These lanes are separated from motor traffic, offering a safer environment for cyclists. The city's cycling lanes are meticulously designed and marked, with distinct bike lanes painted in bright colors, often segregated from pedestrian walkways and motor vehicle lanes. The roads are equipped with bicycle-friendly traffic signals, which help cyclists navigate through intersections efficiently. In many parts of the city, cyclists have their own dedicated traffic lights that give them priority, ensuring smooth flow and reducing waiting times. Furthermore, Copenhagen's city center is particularly accommodating for cyclists. Most streets are bike-accessible, and the roads are designed to promote low-speed, shared environments, which encourage safe cycling even on busier streets. It is not uncommon to see cyclists and pedestrians moving together on wide shared spaces, fostering an integrated cityscape where non-motorized transport reigns.

Bike-Sharing Programs: For visitors who may not have their own bikes, Copenhagen offers several bike-sharing programs that make renting a bike both easy and affordable.

Bycyklen: One of the most popular bike-sharing systems is Bycyklen, the city's electric bike-sharing service. Bycyklen allows users to rent electric bikes at various stations scattered across the city, including in popular tourist areas such as Nyhavn, the City Hall Square, and the Copenhagen Central Station. To rent a Bycyklen, users simply need to download the mobile app, locate a bike, and unlock it via the app. The prices for Bycyklen are typically around DKK 25–35 for a 30-minute ride, with discounts available for longer periods. The app also helps users find nearby charging stations, ensuring that the electric bikes are always ready for use. For more information, you can visit (https://www.bycyklen.dk).

Donkey Republic: In addition to Bycyklen, Donkey Republic is another bike-sharing service in Copenhagen. Donkey Republic operates a fleet of standard bikes that can be unlocked using a mobile app. These bikes are available at numerous locations around the city, and rentals are priced similarly to Bycyklen, generally around DKK 25–40 per hour, with the option to rent bikes for a full day at a discounted rate. Donkey Republic offers the convenience of finding and renting bikes without any interaction with staff, making it a great option for tourists looking for a self-sufficient experience. For more details, visit (https://www.donkey.bike).

Copenhagen City Bikes: For a more traditional bike rental experience, Copenhagen City Bikes offers standard city bikes that can be rented from multiple locations. Prices typically start around DKK 100 for a day's rental, with discounts for longer rental periods. Visit their website at (https://www.citybikes.dk) for more information.

Bike Parking and Storage: Copenhagen is also highly supportive of bike parking. The city has dedicated bike racks throughout its urban areas, ensuring that cyclists can easily park their bikes while visiting shops, restaurants, or tourist attractions. Many of these bike racks are strategically placed in areas of high foot traffic, such as near train stations and shopping streets. For those staying longer in the city or looking for more secure bike storage, Copenhagen offers several underground bike parking facilities. The largest and most notable of these is located near København Central Station, where cyclists can park their bikes in a safe, supervised space for a minimal fee. This facility is ideal for visitors who wish to leave their bikes for an extended period or those looking for extra peace of mind while they explore the city on foot. More information about bike parking facilities can be found on the (https://www.kk.dk/english).

Navigating Copenhagen by Bike: For visitors navigating Copenhagen by bike, the key to a smooth and enjoyable experience is to familiarize themselves with the city's bike infrastructure. One of the first things to know is that cyclists have the right of way in many parts of Copenhagen, including at most traffic lights. This ensures a streamlined, cyclist-centric flow throughout the city. Before venturing out, it's also helpful to download navigation apps that cater to cyclists. Apps like Copenhagen Bike Route Planner provide detailed routes, including bike lanes, shortcuts, and information on bike-friendly roads. These apps are especially useful for those who want to plan their routes efficiently, avoiding areas with heavy traffic and finding the best pathways for scenic ride. For tourists unfamiliar with Copenhagen's layout, it is advisable to stick to the designated bike lanes, which are typically well-marked and provide a safer, more comfortable cycling experience. The city center, in particular, is very well designed for cycling, with dedicated lanes on even the busiest roads. If you're riding in areas less frequented by tourists, such as the outer districts, you'll find that local cyclists are often very friendly and helpful when it comes to navigating the city's cycling infrastructure.

Cycling Etiquette and Safety: While cycling in Copenhagen is generally very safe, it's important for visitors to adhere to basic cycling etiquette. Always yield to pedestrians on shared paths, use hand signals when turning or stopping, and maintain a steady pace. Copenhagen's traffic is bike-centric, but it is still vital to be aware of other cyclists, as the city can get quite busy, especially during rush hours. Cyclists are required by law to wear lights after dark, and it is highly recommended to use a helmet, although wearing one is not mandatory. Lights and reflective vests are available for purchase at local bike shops, and many bike rental services offer them as part of the rental package. For more safety tips, the (https://www.cycling-embassy.dk) offers useful resources and guidelines.

Sustainable Transportation: Copenhagen's commitment to cycling goes beyond just infrastructure. The city has integrated cycling into its larger sustainable transportation plan, aiming to reduce emissions, promote physical health, and create a more accessible environment for people of all ages and abilities. The city's goal is to become the world's first carbon-neutral capital by 2025, and cycling plays a crucial role in this vision. Government initiatives to encourage cycling include subsidies for electric bike purchases, an ongoing expansion of bike lanes, and incentives for businesses to support cycling infrastructure. Copenhagen's bike-sharing services also contribute to this sustainable vision, offering tourists and residents alike an environmentally friendly alternative to car travel.

3.5 Car Rentals and Driving Tips

Renting a car in Copenhagen can be a practical choice for travelers looking to venture beyond the city limits to explore Denmark's picturesque countryside, historic towns, and coastal beauty. While driving in Copenhagen comes with its own set of rules and considerations, understanding the process of renting a car and navigating the city ensures a smooth and enjoyable experience.

Navigating the Car Rental Market in Copenhagen

Copenhagen is home to a range of reputable car rental companies that cater to diverse needs and budgets. International brands and local agencies operate across the city, particularly near major transit hubs such as Copenhagen Airport, central train stations, and key urban locations. These companies offer everything from compact cars for city driving to larger vehicles for families or groups.

Avis: Avis (https://www.avis.dk) has a prominent presence in Copenhagen, with locations at Copenhagen Airport and in the city center. Their fleet includes a wide range of vehicles, and they offer additional services such as GPS rentals and child safety seats. Prices typically start around DKK 500-700 per day for economy cars, with discounts available for weekly rentals.

Hertz: Hertz (https://www.hertz.dk) is another reliable choice, known for its excellent customer service and flexible rental policies. With offices at the airport and in the heart of Copenhagen, Hertz provides an array of vehicles, from economical options to luxury models. Daily rental rates for compact cars begin at approximately DKK 450.

Sixt: Local companies like Sixt (https://www.sixt.dk) and Europcar (https://www.europcar.dk) also operate extensively in Copenhagen, offering competitive prices and convenient pick-up locations. Sixt's airport branch is particularly popular, with rates for standard vehicles starting around DKK 400 per day. Europcar is well-regarded for its transparent pricing and environmentally friendly options, including electric and hybrid cars.

Enterprise: Another noteworthy option is Enterprise Rent-A-Car (https://www.enterprise.dk), which caters to travelers at the airport and several city locations. Enterprise is celebrated for its wide selection of vehicles and customizable rental plans, with daily rates beginning at DKK 500.

Budget: For budget-conscious travelers, Budget Car Rental (https://www.budget.dk) provides economical choices without compromising quality. With multiple branches in Copenhagen, including one at the airport, Budget offers rentals starting as low as DKK 350 per day for compact vehicles.

Essential Information for Renting a Car in Copenhagen

To rent a car in Copenhagen, visitors must meet certain requirements. Drivers need to be at least 21 years old, although some companies impose a higher age requirement for specific vehicle categories or charge a young driver fee for those under 25. A valid driver's license from your home country is essential, and an International Driving Permit (IDP) may be required for licenses not written in Latin characters. When booking a car, it's advisable to make reservations online in advance, especially during peak travel seasons. Booking platforms such as the rental company's official websites or comparison sites like Rentalcars.com (https://www.rentalcars.com) often provide discounts and allow you to compare prices and vehicle availability.

Driving in Copenhagen: Driving in Copenhagen offers freedom and flexibility, but it requires awareness of local traffic rules and customs. Danish roads are well-maintained, and traffic signs are clearly marked, ensuring a smooth driving experience. However, Copenhagen is known for its abundance of cyclists, and drivers must exercise caution to share the road safely. Parking in Copenhagen can be challenging and expensive, especially in the city center. Public parking areas are divided into zones, each with its own pricing and time limits. Blue zones are the most affordable, while red zones are costlier and closer to the city center. Parking meters and apps like EasyPark (https://www.easypark.com) simplify payment. Many hotels also offer parking facilities, which may be included in the room rate or available for an additional fee. Fuel prices in Denmark are relatively high, with petrol costing approximately DKK 15-18 per liter. Most gas stations are self-service and accept credit cards.

Exploring Beyond Copenhagen by Car

Renting a car allows visitors to discover the beauty of Denmark beyond Copenhagen's urban limits. Day trips to destinations like the historic town of Roskilde, home to the Viking Ship Museum, or the scenic North Zealand region with its stunning beaches and castles, are popular options. A drive to the fairy-tale town of Odense, the birthplace of Hans Christian Andersen, offers a delightful glimpse into Danish culture and history. The Danish road network is excellent, with motorways connecting major cities and attractions. The Øresund Bridge, a marvel of modern engineering, provides a direct link to Sweden, making it easy for travelers to extend their adventures into neighboring countries.

3.6 Airport Transfers and Shuttle Services

When arriving at Copenhagen Airport, also known as Kastrup Airport, travelers are greeted with a variety of transfer and shuttle services designed to cater to diverse needs, budgets, and preferences. Navigating these options effectively ensures a smooth transition from the airport to the heart of the city or other destinations in Denmark.

Public Airport Shuttles: One of the most popular ways to travel from Copenhagen Airport to the city center is via public shuttle services. The airport is seamlessly connected to the city's transportation network, making it easy for visitors to hop on a shuttle bus. The Movia network operates several buses, including the 5C, which departs frequently and takes passengers directly to Copenhagen Central Station. Tickets for public buses cost approximately DKK 24–36, depending on the zones covered. These buses run 24/7, offering a reliable and affordable option, especially for budget-conscious travelers. For travelers venturing beyond Copenhagen, regional buses are available from the airport to surrounding towns and cities. While these services are less frequent, they offer a cost-effective solution for exploring the greater Copenhagen area.

Private Airport Transfer Services: Private airport transfer services provide an excellent option for those seeking comfort, privacy, and convenience. These services are ideal for families, business travelers, or individuals with bulky luggage who wish to avoid the hassle of public transport. Companies such as Blacklane, GetTransfer, and Copenhagen Airport Transfer offer tailored experiences with a range of vehicle options, including sedans, SUVs, and luxury cars. Prices for private transfers typically range from DKK 300 to DKK 1,000, depending on the distance and vehicle type. Bookings can be made online in advance, and many providers include perks such as meet-and-greet services, assistance with luggage, and complimentary Wi-Fi during the journey.

Shared Shuttles: For travelers who want to balance cost and convenience, shared shuttle services are an attractive choice. Companies like GoAirport Shuttle and AirPorter offer shared van transfers that pick up multiple passengers heading to similar destinations. This option is more economical than a private transfer, with prices averaging between DKK 150 and DKK 300 per person. Shared shuttles are ideal for solo travelers or small groups and often include door-to-door service, eliminating the need for additional transport upon arrival at your destination. These services usually operate on a fixed schedule, so booking in advance is advisable to secure your seat.

Taxi Services: Taxis provide a flexible and readily available option for airport transfers in Copenhagen. Taxi ranks are conveniently located outside each terminal, and drivers are professional and knowledgeable about the city's layout. Taxis in Copenhagen are metered, with a typical fare to the city center ranging from DKK 250 to DKK 400, depending on traffic and the time of day. Many taxi companies also offer pre-booked airport pick-ups, which can be arranged online or by phone. For added convenience, most vehicles are equipped with card payment systems, ensuring a hassle-free experience for international visitors.

Ride-Sharing Apps: Ride-sharing services such as Uber and Bolt have become increasingly popular in Copenhagen. These apps offer a modern alternative to traditional taxis, often at a slightly lower cost. Travelers can book a ride through the app, which provides an upfront price and estimated arrival time. Depending on the time of day and demand, prices for a ride to the city center typically range from DKK 200 to DKK 350. Ride-sharing apps are especially convenient for tech-savvy visitors who prefer cashless transactions and real-time tracking of their ride.

Navigating Airport Transfers in Copenhagen: To make the most of Copenhagen's airport transfer options, it's essential to plan ahead. Researching and booking transfers in advance not only guarantees availability but also allows travelers to compare prices and services. Upon arrival at the airport, clear signage and helpful staff make it easy to locate your chosen mode of transport. For public transport users, downloading the DOT Mobilbilletter app is highly recommended. This app allows you to purchase tickets for buses, trains, and the metro directly from your smartphone, streamlining your journey. Similarly, private transfer services often provide mobile booking platforms, enabling seamless coordination with drivers. Travelers heading to the city center are advised to consider the metro, which is connected to the airport and offers one of the fastest ways to reach central Copenhagen. Tickets cost approximately DKK 36 and can be purchased at ticket machines or via the app.

CHAPTER 4
TOP 10 ATTRACTIONS & HIDDEN GEMS

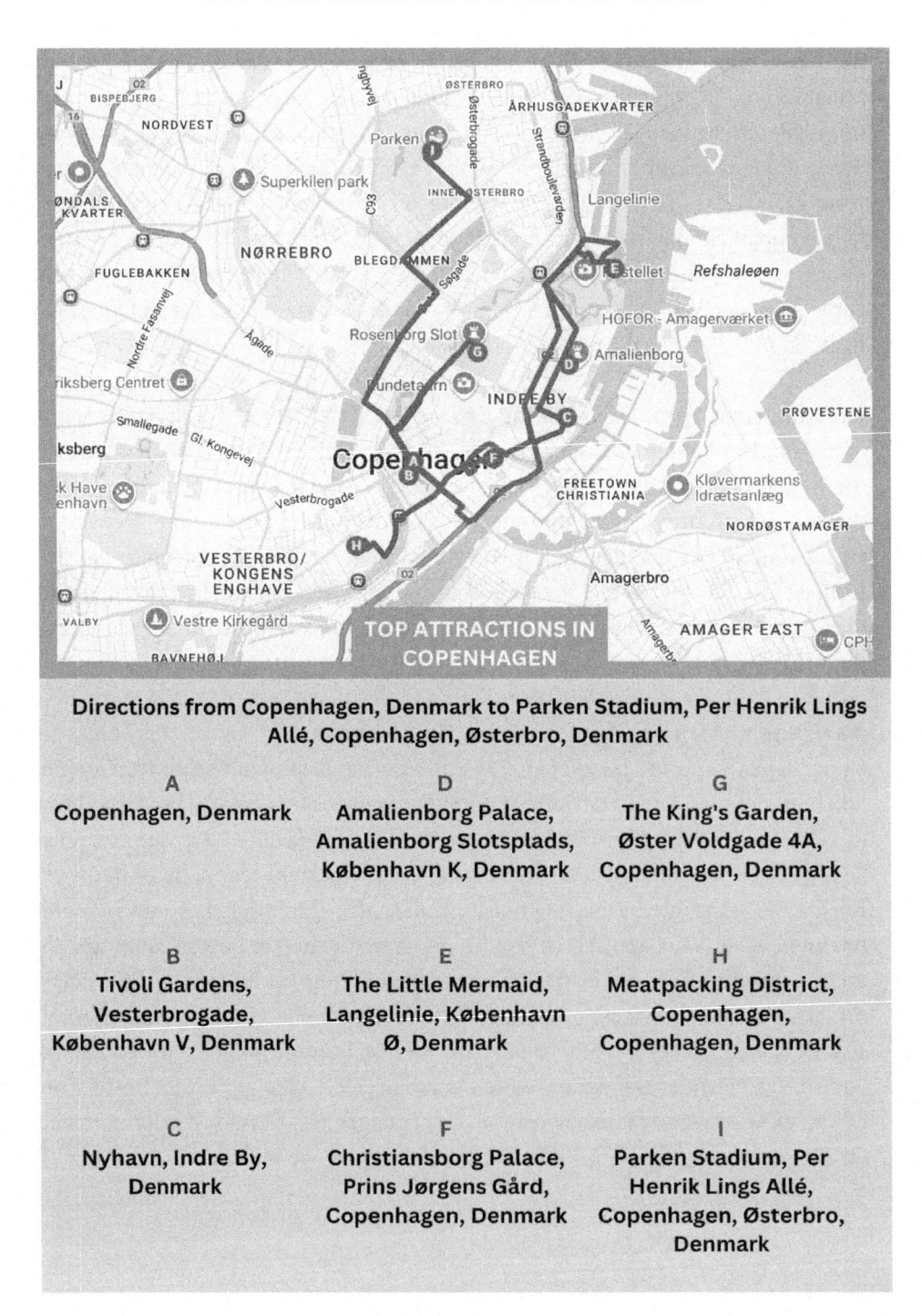

Directions from Copenhagen, Denmark to Parken Stadium, Per Henrik Lings Allé, Copenhagen, Østerbro, Denmark

A
Copenhagen, Denmark

D
Amalienborg Palace, Amalienborg Slotsplads, København K, Denmark

G
The King's Garden, Øster Voldgade 4A, Copenhagen, Denmark

B
Tivoli Gardens, Vesterbrogade, København V, Denmark

E
The Little Mermaid, Langelinie, København Ø, Denmark

H
Meatpacking District, Copenhagen, Copenhagen, Denmark

C
Nyhavn, Indre By, Denmark

F
Christiansborg Palace, Prins Jørgens Gård, Copenhagen, Denmark

I
Parken Stadium, Per Henrik Lings Allé, Copenhagen, Østerbro, Denmark

4.1 Tivoli Gardens and Amusement Park

Tivoli Gardens is not just an amusement park; it's a magical escape where history, thrill, and beauty collide. As one of the world's oldest amusement parks, dating back to 1843, it holds a timeless charm that continues to captivate visitors of all ages. Whether you're a thrill-seeker, a culture enthusiast, or simply someone who loves to bask in enchanting surroundings, Tivoli offers something for everyone. Here are five remarkable places within Tivoli Gardens that will leave you spellbound and eager to explore more.

The Iconic Rutschebanen Roller Coaster: For those who seek an exhilarating ride, the Rutschebanen, or the Wooden Roller Coaster, is a must-try. This classic coaster is not just a ride but a journey through time, being one of the oldest wooden roller coasters in the world. As you feel the rush of wind through your hair and the thrill of the steep drops, you'll experience a unique blend of nostalgia and adrenaline. Built in 1914, the Rutschebanen is as much about the history as it is about the excitement, and its old-world charm is what makes it stand out in an era of high-tech roller coasters. The sounds of laughter, the sharp turns, and the clattering wheels over wooden tracks create an immersive experience that's hard to forget.

The Tivoli Concert Hall: Tivoli Gardens isn't just a place for rides—it's also home to an incredible cultural venue, the Tivoli Concert Hall. This stunning building is where the magic of music meets the ambiance of one of Copenhagen's most historic settings. From classical performances by the Royal Danish Orchestra to contemporary pop concerts, the concert hall offers a variety of performances that add a different layer to your Tivoli visit. The acoustics here are extraordinary, and sitting in the grand hall, surrounded by intricate architecture and soft lighting, will leave you in awe. If you're in the mood for an evening of culture, a concert at Tivoli is an experience you won't want to miss.

The Beautiful Tivoli Gardens' Pavilions: As you stroll through Tivoli Gardens, the many picturesque pavilions that dot the landscape will instantly draw you in. The gardens themselves are a work of art, blending lush greenery, vibrant flowers, and tranquil lakes. However, the pavilions offer a perfect spot to pause and reflect. Each one is unique, from the charming Chinese Pavilion to the elegant Moorish Pavilion, creating an atmospheric setting that invites visitors to relax and immerse themselves in the park's beauty. These pavilions are perfect for taking photos, enjoying a peaceful moment, or simply soaking in the peaceful atmosphere before continuing your adventure.

The Flying Trampolines: For those who are young at heart (or perhaps young in age), the Flying Trampolines are a thrilling, gravity-defying experience that should be on your list. The joy of bouncing high into the air and feeling like you're almost flying is something everyone should try. This nostalgic ride has delighted visitors for generations, and it's not hard to see why. The sense of freedom and exhilaration you feel while soaring above the park, with the entire Tivoli Gardens below you, creates an unforgettable sensation. It's not just a ride; it's a chance to experience the pure joy of flight in one of the most beloved attractions at Tivoli.

The Tivoli Illuminations at Night: One of the most enchanting experiences at Tivoli Gardens occurs when the sun sets and the park transforms into a glowing wonderland. The Tivoli Illuminations, a spectacular light display, turns the entire park into a fairy tale. Thousands of twinkling lights illuminate the rides, pathways, and gardens, casting a magical glow over the entire space. The reflection of the lights in the lakes and the soft, melodic tunes drifting through the air only add to the enchantment.

4.2 Nyhavn Harbour and Colourful Houses

One of the most captivating places in this beautiful city is Nyhavn Harbour, a picturesque waterfront filled with the most iconic and colorful houses. This place offers more than just a postcard-perfect view—it's an invitation to explore, savor, and be inspired by Copenhagen's unique charm. Whether you're strolling along its lively quays or sitting at a café with a coffee in hand, Nyhavn has something to stir your soul. Below are places you must visit while exploring this charming part of Copenhagen:

The Nyhavn Waterfront: Imagine walking along cobbled streets, the salty scent of the sea in the air, and the vibrant reflections of brightly painted buildings shimmering on the water. The Nyhavn waterfront is the perfect place for a leisurely stroll, where the past and present collide. Dating back to the 17th century, Nyhavn was once a bustling port for merchant ships. Today, the old wooden ships docked in the harbor stand as silent witnesses to the transformation of Copenhagen. The surrounding colorful houses, with their red, yellow, and pastel hues, tell tales of bygone days and lively adventures. As you walk along the quay, it's impossible not to feel the magnetism of this historic yet modern area—each step feels like a living snapshot of Copenhagen's spirit.

Canal Boat Tours: For those seeking a deeper connection with Copenhagen's waterways, a canal boat tour from Nyhavn is an absolute must. Stepping onto one of the charming boats, you'll glide through the heart of the city, passing under beautiful bridges and along canals lined with quaint houses. As the boat drifts by, you'll notice how the historical buildings contrast with modern landmarks. The tour is like an introduction to the city, offering glimpses of landmarks like the Opera House, the Little Mermaid statue, and Christiansborg Palace. But it's not just about the sights—it's the unique feeling of being on the water that makes the experience so special. The cool breeze, the sound of water lapping against the boat, and the colorful buildings framing the views make it a magical experience for any traveler.

The Historic Nyhavn District: Beyond the beautiful scenery, Nyhavn Harbour is also a cultural hub. This district has been a melting pot for writers, artists, and musicians throughout the centuries, and its vibrant energy still permeates the area today. One of the most notable figures connected to Nyhavn is Hans Christian Andersen, the beloved Danish fairy-tale author. It is said that he lived in one of the colorful houses along the harbor for a time, and his legacy still echoes through Copenhagen's streets. In fact, you can visit his former residence, which is now marked with a plaque. Beyond the literary history, the streets of Nyhavn are brimming with art galleries, boutiques, and cultural events. Every corner holds a piece of Copenhagen's rich creative heritage.

Dining Along the Quays: Nyhavn is not just a feast for the eyes, but also a paradise for food lovers. With its abundance of waterfront cafes and restaurants, it offers an unrivaled dining experience. Whether you're indulging in traditional Danish dishes like smørrebrød (open-faced sandwiches) or savoring a freshly caught seafood platter, dining by the harbor is an experience that engages all the senses. Picture yourself sitting by the water, the bustling sounds of the harbor in the background, as you enjoy a meal crafted from local ingredients. The vibrant atmosphere of the area, paired with exceptional culinary delights, makes it a place where time slows down, allowing you to savor both the food and the environment around you.

The Iconic 'Minde' Bridge: While the houses of Nyhavn are undoubtedly the main attraction, no visit is complete without crossing the beautiful 'Minde' Bridge, which connects Nyhavn to the nearby Kongens Nytorv. From this vantage point, you'll have one of the best views of the colorful houses lining the waterfront, their vibrant facades glowing in the sunlight or reflecting in the water. This bridge, often brimming with visitors snapping photos, provides the perfect angle for capturing the essence of Nyhavn. The bustling harbor below, the lively crowd, and the colorful buildings make this a quintessential Copenhagen scene. For photographers and those looking to capture a lasting memory, it's an opportunity not to be missed.

4.3 Amalienborg Palace and Royal Guard

Amalienborg Palace is not just a collection of stately buildings—it's a living piece of Danish history. As you approach the palace, you can almost feel the weight of centuries of royal tradition. Situated along the picturesque waterfront, the palace complex consists of four stunning rococo-style buildings, each one a tribute to Denmark's past. The grandeur of Amalienborg is not confined to its architecture alone but is also steeped in the monarchy's legacy. Visitors can experience a sense of awe as they walk through the palace square, particularly during the changing of the guard ceremony. This daily spectacle brings the royal palace to life as the guards, dressed in their iconic red uniforms and tall black bearskin hats, march with precision. The atmosphere is electric, and the sight of the palace, gleaming under the Danish sun, is enough to make you feel like you've stepped back in time. For those lucky enough to enter, the Amalienborg Museum offers an intimate glimpse into royal life. The museum, located in one of the palaces, showcases the luxurious interiors and royal treasures that have been passed down through generations. As you wander through the lavish rooms, it's easy to imagine the Danish royals living their lives here, from state dinners to private moments. It's a rare and powerful connection to a living monarchy.

Changing of the Guard: One of the most captivating experiences in Copenhagen is witnessing the Changing of the Guard at Amalienborg Palace. This centuries-old tradition is more than just a military ceremony—it's a lively and colorful display of Danish pride. Every day at noon, the Royal Guard marches from their barracks at Rosenborg Castle to the palace, flanked by spectators who eagerly anticipate this striking performance. The sound of marching boots fills the air, and the guards' synchronized movements seem almost choreographed. The highlight is when the guards exchange posts at the front of the palace, standing as stoic sentinels to protect the royal family. The ceremony is free and open to the public, making it a must-see for anyone visiting Copenhagen. If you're lucky enough to visit during the summer months, the entire experience is often accompanied by a military band playing traditional Danish tunes, adding a melodic charm to the event.

The Royal Guard's Barracks: Though the Changing of the Guard is a popular spectacle, the Royal Guard's Barracks is a more intimate experience that offers visitors a deeper understanding of the royal security. Located near the iconic Christiansborg Palace, the barracks serve as the home base for Denmark's elite soldiers, who are entrusted with the royal family's safety. Here, visitors can learn about the guard's fascinating history and their essential role in protecting the royal family. The barracks are often less crowded than the palace itself, providing a quiet space to reflect on the duty and discipline required of these soldiers. You may even catch a glimpse of the guards in their daily routines as they prepare for their ceremonial duties, a sight that evokes respect for the service they provide.

The Marble Church: Just across the square from Amalienborg Palace stands the stunning Frederik's Church, more commonly known as the Marble Church. This architectural marvel, with its grand dome and Baroque design, complements the elegance of Amalienborg perfectly. The church's awe-inspiring marble façade reflects the royal splendor, and the interior is just as mesmerizing, with its high, sweeping ceilings and intricate decorations. What makes this church especially significant is its historical connection to the royal family. It was here that Prince Frederick, the future King Frederick VIII, married his beloved Queen Louise in a grand ceremony. Visitors often find themselves lost in the serene atmosphere, staring up at the church's domed ceiling and contemplating the centuries of royal history that have unfolded under its roof. For those seeking quiet reflection after touring Amalienborg, the Marble Church provides a peaceful and majestic sanctuary.

Amalienborg Palace Gardens: After soaking in the regal sights and sounds of Amalienborg Palace, step into the palace gardens to experience a tranquil escape from the hustle and bustle of Copenhagen. These meticulously manicured gardens offer a peaceful retreat, where you can unwind while taking in the panoramic views of the palace and the harbor. The gardens are a serene blend of classical design and natural beauty, with neatly trimmed hedges, flower beds, and fountains that add a touch of elegance. It's the perfect spot for a leisurely stroll or to sit and reflect on the royal heritage that surrounds you. Whether you're seeking a quiet moment to yourself or a picturesque backdrop for photos, the Amalienborg Palace Gardens offer a gentle, peaceful atmosphere that contrasts beautifully with the grandeur of the palace itself.

4.4 The Little Mermaid and Waterfront

Copenhagen's iconic symbol, the Little Mermaid statue, stands poised and graceful on a rock at the entrance to the city's harbor. While her small size might be unexpected for first-time visitors, her historical and emotional significance resonates deeply. Erected in 1913 and inspired by Hans Christian Andersen's beloved fairy tale, this bronze statue portrays the melancholic mermaid yearning to join the human world. As you stand before her, with the wind gently rustling her hair and the soft ripple of the water around her, you can't help but feel a poignant connection to the themes of love, sacrifice, and longing. It's a moment of reflection, a piece of art that speaks to everyone who passes by, no matter their background. To experience the Little Mermaid is to stand at the edge of an eternal story, waiting to be retold.

Langelinie Promenade: Just a short walk from the Little Mermaid, the Langelinie Promenade offers a peaceful retreat where you can take in the beauty of Copenhagen's waterfront. The wide path stretches along the water's edge, providing stunning views of the harbor, the nearby ships, and the vast horizon beyond. As you stroll, the cool sea breeze invites relaxation while the scent of saltwater and the sight of sailboats gently gliding by add to the charm. This waterfront oasis is not just about scenic beauty; it's also a place to pause and reflect on Copenhagen's maritime history. The promenade, with its lush green spaces, also leads you to nearby attractions like the Kastellet, a historic star-shaped fortress, making it a perfect destination for those who want a quiet escape in the heart of the city.

Nyhavn: A visit to Nyhavn, Copenhagen's most picturesque harbor, is nothing short of magical. As you approach this lively canal, you are greeted by brightly colored buildings that line the waterway, each one steeped in centuries of history. Originally a bustling center of trade, Nyhavn today is a lively hub of restaurants, bars, and outdoor cafés. Here, you can sip on a cold Danish beer while watching boats sail by, or take a boat tour through the city's canals to see Copenhagen from a different angle. The vibrant atmosphere of Nyhavn, combined with its stunning backdrop of historic ships and old warehouses, creates an unforgettable experience. Whether you're visiting in the summer, when the area is filled with life, or in the winter, when the lights and decorations create a cozy, magical vibe, Nyhavn is the heartbeat of Copenhagen's waterfront.

The Royal Danish Playhouse: For those with an appreciation for the arts, the Royal Danish Playhouse (Skuespilhuset) is an architectural masterpiece situated right on the water's edge. With its sleek modern design and stunning glass walls, the Playhouse offers breathtaking views of both the harbor and the city skyline. Home to the Royal Danish Theatre, this venue stages a variety of performances, from classic plays to contemporary productions. But even if you're not catching a show, the Playhouse is worth a visit for its ambiance alone. The surrounding area offers a tranquil escape, with outdoor seating by the water perfect for watching the sunset. Whether you're exploring the arts or simply enjoying the waterfront, the Royal Danish Playhouse is an inspiring place to pause and soak in Copenhagen's creative energy.

Amalienborg Palace: A short distance from the Little Mermaid lies Amalienborg Palace, the stunning royal residence that sits gracefully by the water. The palace complex, made up of four grand buildings surrounding a central square, is home to Denmark's royal family. As you walk through the cobblestone streets of the square, you'll be transported to a world of regal elegance. Amalienborg is especially famous for its changing of the guard ceremony, which takes place daily and offers a unique opportunity to witness a long-standing royal tradition. The view from the square, with its proximity to the waterfront, adds a special charm to the experience. The palace's rich history and breathtaking architecture make it one of Copenhagen's most enchanting landmarks. Whether you're interested in royal history or simply captivated by the beauty of the palace's surroundings, Amalienborg Palace offers a glimpse into Denmark's storied past.

4.5 National Museum of Denmark and History

The National Museum of Denmark (Nationalmuseet) stands as a testament to the country's rich history, culture, and evolving identity. Located in the heart of Copenhagen, this museum is more than just a collection of artifacts—it's a time machine that transports visitors through Denmark's past, from the prehistoric era to the present day. Whether you're an art lover, history buff, or curious traveler, the museum's diverse exhibits promise a deeply engaging experience. Here are incredible places within the museum that will ignite your curiosity and captivate your imagination.

The Prehistoric Denmark Exhibit: Step into Denmark's ancient past with the Prehistoric Denmark exhibit, where you can trace the country's human history from its very earliest inhabitants. This exhibit is a journey through time, where you'll encounter fascinating displays of tools, weapons, and ceremonial objects used by Denmark's early peoples. The pièce de résistance here is the famous

Sun Chariot, a magnificent Bronze Age relic that will undoubtedly leave you in awe. As you explore, you'll gain a deep sense of connection to the land's first settlers, understanding their struggles, triumphs, and ways of life. The exhibit's immersive atmosphere and carefully curated artifacts invite you to imagine what life must have been like thousands of years ago.

The Viking Exhibition: Few periods of history evoke as much fascination as the Viking Age, and the National Museum offers an unforgettable look at this remarkable era through its Viking exhibition. The exhibit brings to life the bold and adventurous spirit of the Vikings, exploring their seafaring expeditions, their elaborate burial customs, and their vast influence on Europe. Highlights include real Viking ships, preserved skeletal remains, intricate weapons, and beautifully crafted jewelry. But beyond the artifacts, the exhibit paints a vivid picture of Viking culture, allowing you to step into their world of warriors, explorers, and traders. It's a place where the ancient stories of Odin, Thor, and the great Viking chieftains feel real and tangible.

The Danish Middle Ages Exhibit: The Danish Middle Ages exhibit at the National Museum offers a fascinating glimpse into Denmark's development during one of its most turbulent and transformative periods. In this section, visitors can explore the daily lives of people in medieval Denmark—noblemen, peasants, and clergy alike. The exhibit features an impressive collection of medieval artwork, tools, and religious artifacts. Among the most striking pieces is the Erlingsen altarpiece, a stunning example of medieval craftsmanship that will leave you marveling at its intricate details. Walking through this exhibit, you'll witness the rise of castles, the spread of Christianity, and the changing dynamics of power and society that laid the groundwork for modern Denmark.

The Royal Danish Treasures: For those with an interest in royalty, the National Museum's collection of Royal Danish Treasures is nothing short of mesmerizing. This exhibit is a celebration of Denmark's royal heritage, showcasing exquisite items belonging to Danish monarchs over the centuries. From ornate crowns and scepters to opulent gowns and jewels, these treasures reflect the grandeur and prestige of Denmark's monarchy. The exhibit not only tells the story of the royal family's rise and influence but also provides an intimate look at the personal lives of kings and queens, giving visitors a deeper understanding of the country's royal history. Standing in front of the crowns worn by Denmark's monarchs or gazing at royal portraits, you'll be transported into a world of power, elegance, and history.

The World Culture Exhibition: Beyond Denmark, the National Museum also invites you to explore the fascinating cultures of the world. The World Culture exhibition showcases artifacts and treasures from far-off lands, including Africa, Asia, and the Americas. This section is a stunning representation of humanity's shared history and diverse traditions. From the delicate craftsmanship of Asian porcelain to the bold artistry of African tribal masks, this exhibit celebrates the richness of global heritage. It's a place where you can expand your horizons, understanding the connections between cultures and seeing the world through a different lens. The immersive displays and thought-provoking artifacts will leave you with a profound appreciation for the beauty and diversity of human civilization.

4.6 Christiansborg Palace and Parliament

In the heart of Copenhagen stands Christiansborg Palace, a magnificent blend of royal history, political power, and architectural grandeur. This landmark is not only a testament to Denmark's royal past but also a vibrant center of governance and culture today. As you step through its imposing gates, you're not just entering a palace—you're stepping into centuries of history that still resonate in the halls, chambers, and chambers of power. Here are must-visit places within Christiansborg Palace and its surrounding complex, each offering a unique perspective of Denmark's rich heritage.

The Royal Reception Rooms: Imagine walking through the grand, gilded halls once frequented by kings and queens. The Royal Reception Rooms are a majestic journey through Denmark's royal heritage. These opulent rooms are where the Danish monarchy still conducts official state affairs, and they exude the power and elegance of a bygone era. The spaces are lavishly decorated with intricate tapestries, grand chandeliers, and royal insignia that transport you back in time. The most striking feature is the Throne Room, a stunning chamber that has been used for royal ceremonies since the 19th century. The rich gold and blue hues of the room, combined with its regal decor, offer a rare and intimate glimpse into Denmark's royal world.

The Parliament Chambers: For those intrigued by the pulse of Denmark's political heart, the Parliament Chambers offer an incredible opportunity to witness the workings of democracy in action. Christiansborg is home to the Folketinget, Denmark's parliament, and the chambers within the palace are where laws are debated and passed. A visit to the Folketinget is a rare chance to witness the political process up close, whether by attending a live session or simply admiring the dignified space. The chambers are filled with a sense of history, as well as a palpable energy that signifies Denmark's forward-thinking approach to governance. If you're lucky, you may even catch a glimpse of the politicians themselves, debating on matters that shape the future of Denmark.

The Royal Stables: Tucked away beneath the grandiose palace is the Royal Stables, a place where royal tradition and power come to life. Though the Danish royal family no longer uses the stables for everyday travel, they remain an important piece of the country's history. The stables are home to the famous Royal Life Guards, who have served as protectors of the monarchy for centuries. The stables themselves are a marvel of design, with their airy ceilings and intricate woodwork, showcasing the craftsmanship of a bygone era. The Royal Stables Exhibition allows visitors to explore the role horses played in Danish royal life, with a collection of royal carriages, uniforms, and fascinating artifacts on display. It's a place that combines regal pomp with the working-life of Denmark's royal family, making it an unforgettable part of any visit.

The Palace Chapel: Located within the heart of Christiansborg Palace is the Palace Chapel, a serene and elegant sanctuary that contrasts beautifully with the grandeur of its surroundings. Though it is often overshadowed by the larger, more public areas of the palace, this chapel holds a deeply spiritual significance.

The chapel has been the site of many royal weddings, christenings, and other religious ceremonies, making it a place of both royal and national importance. The stained-glass windows, the intricate woodwork, and the peaceful atmosphere make it an ideal place for reflection amid the bustling political and royal activities just outside. The chapel's quiet grace is a reminder of the delicate balance between power and faith in Denmark's history.

The Christiansborg Palace Tower: No visit to Christiansborg is complete without ascending the Palace Tower, the tallest building in central Copenhagen. From here, you can enjoy a breathtaking panoramic view of the city. On a clear day, the views stretch from the bustling streets of the city center to the glittering waters of the harbor, and even as far as the iconic Little Mermaid statue and the green expanses of Amager Fælled park. The tower offers a rare, bird's-eye view of Copenhagen's landscape, providing a refreshing break from the historical spaces below. The tower's open-air viewing platform invites visitors to pause, take in the sights, and reflect on the rich tapestry of culture, politics, and history that defines this captivating city.

4.7 Rosenborg Castle and Gardens

Rosenborg Castle stands as a stunning testament to Denmark's royal history, its towering spires and beautiful brickwork drawing visitors into a world of opulence and grandeur. Built in the early 17th century by King Christian IV, the castle offers a truly immersive experience for anyone with an appreciation for history and architecture. As you approach the castle, its fairytale-like appearance, with intricate turrets and a moat that reflects its regal stature, instantly transports you into the past. Inside, Rosenborg is an absolute treasure trove. The rooms are brimming with royal artifacts, from the majestic coronation thrones to the dazzling array of royal portraits that hang in nearly every chamber. As you wander through the castle's grand halls, you can almost feel the presence of the monarchs who once walked these floors. For those captivated by royal opulence, Rosenborg Castle offers an unfiltered, up-close look at Denmark's rich history, with the added bonus of stunning views over the surrounding city.

The Crown Jewels: One of the most compelling reasons to visit Rosenborg Castle is the chance to see the magnificent collection of Danish crown jewels, which are housed in the castle's Lower Chamber. These jewels, which include coronation regalia, royal scepters, and the famous crown worn by Denmark's monarchs, shimmer with an almost otherworldly glow. The room itself is designed to highlight the magnificence of these treasures, with dim lighting and displays that emphasize the intricate craftsmanship of each piece. It's not just the size and beauty of the jewels that captivate, but the history behind them. These sacred objects have been used in royal ceremonies for centuries, and as you stand before them, you can't help but feel the weight of tradition and the sense of power they symbolize. The presence of the jewels in their original setting allows visitors to truly connect with Denmark's royal heritage in a way that's both intimate and awe-inspiring.

The King's Chamber: One of the most enchanting rooms in Rosenborg Castle is the King's Chamber, which reflects the wealth and sophistication of its former inhabitants. Designed as a place for King Christian IV to retreat from the public eye, this space exudes a sense of luxury and refinement. The room's rich tapestries, grand furniture, and opulent decor bring to life the daily routines of a royal king. Standing in this chamber, you can almost imagine the monarch in his royal regalia, surrounded by courtiers and advisors. It's a room that tells the story of a king who shaped Denmark's history with his vision and authority. The attention to detail in this room—whether it's the gold-framed mirrors or the elaborate fireplace—speaks volumes about the level of prestige associated with the Danish monarchy. Visiting the King's Chamber offers an intimate connection to the life of the royals and gives you a rare glimpse into the luxury they once enjoyed.

The Castle Gardens: While Rosenborg Castle itself is a marvel to explore, the castle gardens provide the perfect counterpoint—a tranquil retreat where visitors can relax and take in the beauty of nature. Situated behind the castle, the gardens are a splendid example of Renaissance landscaping, with geometric flower beds, manicured lawns, and shaded pathways. It's easy to lose track of time here, whether you're wandering along the flower-lined paths or sitting by one of the decorative fountains. The gardens are an oasis of calm in the heart of Copenhagen, providing visitors with an opportunity to reflect on the majesty of the castle while surrounded by nature's beauty. In the warmer months, the gardens come alive with vibrant colors, and the aroma of blooming flowers fills the air. Whether you're simply enjoying a quiet moment or taking photos of the picturesque surroundings, the castle gardens are an essential part of the Rosenborg experience.

The Knight's Hall: For anyone fascinated by history and warfare, the Knight's Hall in Rosenborg Castle is an absolute must-see. This impressive room houses an extensive collection of royal armor, including some of the most beautiful and intricate pieces from Denmark's military past. From gleaming breastplates to intricately designed helmets, each item tells a story of battles fought and victories won. The Knight's Hall is not only a room filled with awe-inspiring armor but also a place where visitors can learn about Denmark's military history and the role the royal family played in shaping the country's defense. The craftsmanship of the armor is astounding, with many pieces featuring elaborate engravings and gold accents that reflect the wealth and status of the royals who wore them. Standing among these magnificent pieces, it's easy to imagine the kings and knights of old, donning their armor in preparation for battle, their courage and resolve etched in every curve of the metal.

4.8 Vesterbro and Meatpacking District

The Meatpacking District, or Kødbyen, in Vesterbro is a former industrial area that has undergone an incredible transformation into one of Copenhagen's most dynamic and creative neighborhoods. Walking through Kødbyen, you are enveloped by a blend of old-world charm and modern innovation. The streets are lined with repurposed warehouses that now house contemporary art galleries, trendy cafés, buzzing nightclubs, and artisan food markets. By day, the area is a haven for food lovers and art enthusiasts alike, with boutique eateries offering everything from gourmet burgers to innovative Nordic cuisine. As evening falls, the district comes alive with a vibrant nightlife scene, where music spills out from underground clubs and the energy is palpable. Visiting Kødbyen is more than just a trip to a neighborhood—it's stepping into a cultural movement that blends history, creativity, and a sense of community.

Vesterbro's "Grønne Lade": While the Meatpacking District may capture most of Vesterbro's attention, Grønne Lade, a lush green space tucked away near the old railway tracks, offers a peaceful escape for those seeking a quiet moment in nature. This hidden gem is a quiet park where locals come to relax, walk dogs, or just enjoy the outdoors. The surrounding area, once home to Copenhagen's bustling meat industry, is now home to trendy cafes and modern apartments that reflect the neighborhood's evolving character. But Grønne Lade remains an oasis of calm—a space where the city's relentless pace slows down for a while, giving you a rare opportunity to breathe in the fresh air and appreciate the juxtaposition of green space and urban life.

Vesterbro's Street Art and Murals: Vesterbro is a canvas of creativity, and nowhere is this more evident than in its vibrant street art scene. From towering murals on the sides of buildings to intricate graffiti adorning alleyways, the neighborhood is a visual journey into Copenhagen's most avant-garde culture. Artists from all over the world have left their mark on the district, turning ordinary streets into a living, breathing art gallery. Walking through these streets feels like stepping into a dynamic conversation between the city's past and present. The walls whisper stories of rebellion, freedom, and expression. For those with a keen eye for art or simply a desire to explore, Vesterbro's street art is an ever-changing testament to the neighborhood's creative pulse.

Enghave Park: In the heart of Vesterbro, Enghave Park offers a moment of respite from the urban hustle. Whether you're sitting on a bench watching the locals play frisbee or taking a quiet walk by the pond, Enghave Park has an inviting atmosphere that makes it easy to forget you're in the middle of a bustling city. The park's charm is in its simplicity—well-maintained lawns, shaded paths, and plenty of space for picnics or quiet reflection. The surrounding area is a beautiful blend of old Copenhagen and new, with stylish buildings that overlook the park's greenery. In the summertime, the park becomes a gathering place for families, young professionals, and visitors alike, offering a slice of tranquility that invites you to slow down and savor the moment.

Vesterbro's Retro Bars and Cafés: Vesterbro is known for its cool, quirky vibe, and the retro bars and cafés that line its streets are a perfect reflection of this unique atmosphere. These vintage-inspired hangouts transport you back in time, with their old-school interiors, classic cocktails, and cozy ambiance. Whether you find yourself sipping a cocktail in a speakeasy-style bar or enjoying a cup of artisanal coffee in a café with mid-century décor, these spots offer a perfect blend of nostalgia and modernity. Vesterbro's retro scene isn't just about the décor—it's about the experience.

4.9 Østerbro and Parken Stadium

The vibrant district of Østerbro and the iconic Parken Stadium are two of Copenhagen's gems that promise unforgettable experiences. Whether you're drawn to natural beauty, sporting excitement, or a glimpse into local life, this neighborhood has something for every traveler. Here are exceptional places within Østerbro and Parken Stadium that will leave you eager to explore more.

Fælledparken: Fælledparken, one of the largest and most beloved parks in Copenhagen, is a tranquil retreat in the heart of Østerbro. This lush green oasis offers an escape from the hustle and bustle of the city, making it a perfect spot for relaxation and outdoor activities. With its expansive lawns, peaceful lakes, and winding pathways, Fælledparken invites visitors to explore its serene beauty. Whether you're enjoying a leisurely picnic, walking along the tree-lined paths, or simply lying on the grass soaking up the atmosphere, Fælledparken feels like a breath of fresh air in the heart of Copenhagen. For those with a penchant for sports, the park also offers tennis courts, football fields, and outdoor fitness equipment, adding a touch of activity to the peaceful environment.

Parken Stadium: For sports enthusiasts, Parken Stadium is undoubtedly the crown jewel of Østerbro. As the home of Denmark's national football team, this iconic stadium pulsates with energy on match days, making it a must-see for anyone visiting Copenhagen. The stadium itself is an architectural marvel, with a sleek design that combines modernity with tradition. Whether you're attending a football match, a concert, or a special event, the atmosphere at Parken is electric, and the crowd's passion for their team is infectious. Even if you're not in town for a game, a tour of the stadium allows you to get an inside look at one of the most prestigious sporting venues in Denmark. Standing in the stands or on the pitch itself, you can almost feel the intensity of the matches played here.

Østerbro's Charming Streets and Cafes: Østerbro's streets are a reflection of Copenhagen's laid-back yet vibrant atmosphere. Lined with a mix of modern boutiques, local shops, and cozy cafés, wandering through Østerbro feels like stepping into a true Danish neighborhood. Among its picturesque streets, you'll find charming cafés where you can enjoy a traditional Danish pastry, sip on a coffee, or savor a hearty brunch. The district has an effortlessly cool vibe, with a mix of local residents and visitors blending seamlessly in the cafes, shops, and art galleries. A leisurely stroll through Østerbro will give you a glimpse into the daily life of Copenhagen's residents and leave you with a genuine appreciation for the city's relaxed yet stylish pace.

The Little Mermaid: Though technically just outside Østerbro, the iconic Little Mermaid statue is only a short walk from the district and should be on every visitor's list. This world-famous statue, perched on a rock by the water, is a symbol of Denmark's maritime heritage and one of Copenhagen's most photographed landmarks. While its small size might surprise first-time visitors, the beauty of the statue lies in its serene expression and the enchanting story behind it. Inspired by Hans Christian Andersen's beloved fairy tale, the Little Mermaid has become a symbol of Denmark's rich literary and cultural tradition. A visit here is an essential part of experiencing Copenhagen, offering an iconic photo opportunity and a connection to the city's artistic soul.

4.10 Frederiksberg and Gardens

Frederiksberg is home to lush green spaces, grand avenues, and fascinating cultural gems that offer visitors a serene escape from the hustle and bustle. Whether you're seeking to relax in nature, indulge in local delicacies, or explore Denmark's royal heritage, Frederiksberg has something to enchant you. Below are places in Frederiksberg that should be on every traveler's list.

Frederiksberg Gardens: One of the most captivating spots in the Frederiksberg area is undoubtedly the Frederiksberg Gardens. This expansive and meticulously designed park offers visitors a peaceful retreat from the urban frenzy. As you walk along the winding paths, you'll be enveloped in the beauty of manicured lawns, elegant fountains, and charming canals. The park's centerpiece is the majestic Frederiksberg Palace, which sits proudly on a hill overlooking the gardens. The historical charm of the palace combined with the serene beauty of the park creates an idyllic setting for a leisurely stroll or a relaxing afternoon picnic. Don't miss the Chinese Pavilion, an exotic and whimsical structure nestled by the water, offering an air of mystery and intrigue.

Copenhagen Zoo: Adjacent to the Frederiksberg Gardens, Copenhagen Zoo is one of the oldest and most beloved zoos in Europe. The zoo offers an immersive experience for families, animal lovers, and anyone with an interest in wildlife. As you walk through its beautifully designed enclosures, you'll encounter a wide variety of animals from around the world, including elephants, tigers, and polar bears. The zoo's most iconic structure is the Zoological Garden's Elephant House, a striking architectural gem designed by famed Danish architect Norman Foster. The house is a marvel of modern design and is an excellent example of how architecture and nature can blend seamlessly. The zoo's lush, spacious grounds provide not only a chance to view incredible wildlife but also a chance to unwind amidst the beauty of Frederiksberg's green spaces.

The Frederiksberg Alle: For those looking to experience the local charm of Frederiksberg, the Frederiksberg Alle is a must-visit. This elegant boulevard, lined with towering trees and beautiful 19th-century buildings, is one of the most picturesque streets in Copenhagen. As you stroll along the alle, you'll pass stylish cafes, boutique shops, and charming cafes that exude a quintessentially Copenhagen atmosphere. The energy of the street is laid-back yet vibrant, making it the perfect place to stop for a coffee or enjoy a leisurely lunch while soaking in the views. Frederiksberg Alle also offers glimpses of the district's rich history, with its beautifully preserved architecture offering a taste of old-world Copenhagen.

The Royal Copenhagen Bowling Hall: For a more unique experience, make your way to The Royal Copenhagen Bowling Hall. Located near Frederiksberg, this historic venue is one of the oldest bowling alleys in the world, offering a nostalgic experience for anyone who enjoys a bit of fun and history combined. The hall's traditional wooden lanes and cozy atmosphere transport you back to a different era when bowling was a favorite pastime of the Danish elite. Whether you're a seasoned bowler or just looking for something different to do, this charming spot provides a delightful, unexpected adventure in the heart of Frederiksberg.

The Frederiksberg Church: Tucked away amidst the green surroundings of Frederiksberg is the stunning Frederiksberg Church, one of Copenhagen's hidden architectural gems. This neoclassical church is a peaceful retreat, known for its serene interior, grand columns, and beautiful altar. The church is an example of architectural elegance, and its design reflects the refined taste of the 18th century. Visitors can take a moment to marvel at the church's intricate details or simply enjoy the calming atmosphere within. The Frederiksberg

Church's peaceful vibe, combined with its history, makes it the perfect spot to pause and reflect during your exploration of the area.

4.11 Outdoor Activities and Adventures

Copenhagen has something for every type of adventurer. From cycling along scenic paths to experiencing the wind on your face during windsurfing, the city's outdoor offerings are as diverse as they are captivating. In this guide, we explore five of the best sports, outdoor activities, and adventures in Copenhagen, each offering its own set of unique features, locations, and services that promise to make your visit memorable.

Cycling Around Copenhagen: Copenhagen is renowned for being one of the most bike-friendly cities in the world, and cycling here is both a way of life and an exhilarating outdoor adventure. The city boasts an extensive network of well-maintained bike lanes, making it easy for cyclists to navigate its streets, parks, and scenic waterfronts. Visitors can rent bikes from various rental services around the city, with prices typically ranging from 100 to 150 DKK per day, depending on the type of bike you choose. One of the most unique features of cycling in Copenhagen is the ability to rent bikes through the city's bike-share programs like Donkey Republic, which offers flexible pricing based on your usage, and Bycyklen, the city's official bike-sharing service. Both services allow tourists to pick up and drop off bikes at numerous convenient locations, ensuring that you can explore the city at your own pace. Cycling is more than just a means of getting from point A to point B in Copenhagen—it's a journey through the city's iconic neighborhoods, stunning parks, and along the waterfront. Take a leisurely ride through Fælledparken, Copenhagen's largest park, or along the scenic Søndermarken and Vesterbro, soaking in the charming architecture and vibrant street life. For a more adventurous ride, head towards the waterfront, where the cool breeze and picturesque harbor views offer a peaceful yet invigorating experience. To make the most of your cycling experience, many rental services offer guided cycling tours, providing you with insight into Copenhagen's rich history and architecture while riding through its streets. For more information on bike rentals, visit Bycyklen at (https://www.bycyklen.dk) and Donkey Republic at (https://www.donkey.bike).

Windsurfing and Water Sports at Amager Strandpark: For those seeking a more exhilarating outdoor activity, windsurfing at Amager Strandpark is a must-try. Located just a short distance from the city center, Amager Strandpark is one of Copenhagen's most popular beaches, offering a perfect setting for water sports. The park stretches over 4.6 kilometers of coastline, featuring shallow waters and consistent winds, which makes it an ideal spot for both beginners and experienced windsurfers alike. Windsurfing lessons are available at Copenhagen Surf School, with prices starting at around 400 DKK per hour for a group lesson or 600 DKK for a private session. The school provides all the necessary equipment, including boards and sails, ensuring that visitors can enjoy a safe and enjoyable experience. Amager Strandpark's charm goes beyond windsurfing—this coastal area is also a haven for kayaking, stand-up paddleboarding (SUP), and even sailing. The calm waters of the harbor make it a great place for those who want to try paddleboarding or kayaking, with rentals available for around 100-150 DKK per hour. For a more immersive experience, consider joining one of the guided tours offered by Kulturhavn (Copenhagen's cultural harbor tours) for an opportunity to explore the city from the water. This area is a true paradise for water sports enthusiasts, offering an exciting escape from the city's urban bustle. For more information, visit Copenhagen Surf School at (https://www.copenhagensurfschool.com).

Kayaking and Canoeing Through Copenhagen's Canals: Copenhagen's picturesque canals offer an entirely different adventure for those looking to explore the city's beauty from the water. Kayaking or canoeing through these serene waterways gives visitors the chance to glide past the city's historic architecture, picturesque bridges, and vibrant neighborhoods. One of the most popular locations for kayaking is the Copenhagen Canal, where you can rent a kayak from local rental companies such as Kayak Republic or Canoe Copenhagen. Rentals start at around 200 DKK per hour, with discounts available for longer rentals or group bookings. The waterways of Copenhagen are calm and easy to navigate, making it suitable for both beginners and more experienced paddlers. As you paddle through the canals, you'll pass landmarks such as the iconic Nyhavn, the vibrant district famous for its colorful houses and bustling cafés, and Christianshavn, home to the innovative modern architecture of The Opera House. Kayak tours are also available, where expert guides will take you on a journey through the canals, sharing fascinating stories and historical insights about Copenhagen's rich maritime heritage. This activity offers an unforgettable way to explore the city from a completely new perspective. For more information, visit Kayak Republic at (https://www.kayakrepublic.dk).

Urban Climbing at the CopenHill: For those looking to add a thrilling edge to their outdoor activities, urban climbing at CopenHill is an experience unlike any other. CopenHill is Copenhagen's iconic waste-to-energy plant that has been transformed into an urban adventure park with a climbing wall that takes you to the top of the building. The climbing wall, which is a part of the facility's roof, offers spectacular views over the city as climbers ascend through various levels of difficulty. The CopenHill also features a ski slope on its roof for year-round activities, making it one of the most unique places in the world where you can combine nature, sustainability, and adventure in one experience. Urban climbing at CopenHill is not only for experienced climbers; the facility offers courses for beginners and climbing enthusiasts of all skill levels. Prices for a climbing session start at around 300 DKK per person for a guided session, and equipment is provided. The unique aspect of this activity is its commitment to sustainability—CopenHill's efforts to recycle and transform waste into energy reflect Denmark's progressive approach to eco-friendly urban living. After climbing, you can relax on the facility's rooftop, taking in panoramic views of Copenhagen and its surrounding landscapes. For more information, visit CopenHill at (https://www.copenhill.dk).

Hiking and Exploring the Green Trails of Dyrehaven: For those who prefer a slower pace, Dyrehaven, Copenhagen's stunning royal deer park, offers a perfect hiking destination just north of the city center. This vast, ancient forest is home to roaming deer and offers miles of picturesque trails for hikers of all abilities. The park's serene atmosphere, coupled with its rich history and natural beauty, makes it an ideal place to reconnect with nature while still being close to the city. The park is free to visit, and it's open year-round, with different trails that lead visitors through dense woodlands, open meadows, and along tranquil lakes. Hiking here is not just about exercise; it's about immersing yourself in Copenhagen's natural environment, taking in the sight of grazing deer, and perhaps even spotting some of the 200 species of birds that call the park home. For a more guided experience, Dyrehaven's Visitor Center offers nature tours and educational programs about the park's history and wildlife. This activity is perfect for those looking to spend a peaceful day outdoors, away from the hustle and bustle of city life. Prices for guided tours start at around 150 DKK per person, depending on the tour type. Dyrehaven is accessible by public transportation, and visitors can easily spend a few hours wandering its expansive grounds. For more information, visit the official website at www.danmarkshistorien.dk.

4.12 Guided Tours and Recommended Tour Operators

Whether you're fascinated by the royal history, curious about its modern design, or eager to explore hidden gems off the beaten path, the city's expert tour operators are here to enrich your experience. Each tour operator brings something unique to the table, from historical insights to personalized experiences. Here's a closer look at Copenhagen's most recommended tour operators and guided tours, offering a range of experiences designed to make your visit unforgettable.

Copenhagen Bike Tours: Copenhagen is widely known for its cycling culture, and what better way to explore this bike-friendly city than with Copenhagen Bike Tours. This tour operator, based in the heart of the city, specializes in guided bicycle tours that take you through the city's most iconic sights while providing fascinating historical context along the way. Their tours are perfect for those who want to experience Copenhagen at a leisurely pace, soaking in the sights and sounds from the comfort of a bicycle. One of the standout features of Copenhagen Bike Tours is their focus on eco-friendly travel. They offer a range of bikes to suit every preference, including classic city bikes, e-bikes, and even tandem bikes for couples or friends. The company offers various tour options, such as the Classic Copenhagen Tour, which covers major attractions like Nyhavn, Christiansborg Palace, and the Little Mermaid statue, with prices starting around DKK 350 per person for a 3-hour guided ride. Another popular option is the Copenhagen Food Tour by Bike, which combines cycling with culinary exploration, allowing visitors to taste some of the city's finest street food while biking through the neighborhoods. The tours are led by knowledgeable and friendly guides, often locals, who share intriguing facts and stories about Copenhagen's history and culture. They cater to cyclists of all skill levels, ensuring a relaxed, enjoyable experience. For more details, you can visit their official website at www.copenhagenbiketours.com.

Wonderful Copenhagen: When it comes to comprehensive and authentic guided tours, Wonderful Copenhagen is the city's official tourism organization, offering a wide range of curated experiences. As a visitor, you can rest assured that the services offered by Wonderful Copenhagen are of the highest quality, with expert local guides who are passionate about showing off the best of the city. Wonderful Copenhagen provides an assortment of walking and bus tours that are ideal for first-time visitors. One of the most notable tours is the

Copenhagen Grand Tour, a 4-hour tour that combines a bus ride and a walking tour, allowing visitors to see a combination of famous landmarks and hidden gems. With prices starting around DKK 495, this tour covers everything from the royal palaces to the charming streets of the Latin Quarter, ensuring that no major sight is left out. In addition to their regular tours, Wonderful Copenhagen also offers private tours for groups or families, allowing for a more personalized experience. Their special services include multilingual guides, transportation services, and even themed tours, such as architecture tours or sustainable travel experiences. The official website at www.wonderfulcopenhagen.dk is an excellent resource for booking tours and discovering the wide variety of experiences they offer.

Segway Tours Copenhagen: For those looking for a more modern and exhilarating way to explore Copenhagen, Segway Tours Copenhagen offers a fun alternative to traditional walking tours. Located near the city center, this operator specializes in guided Segway tours, providing a unique way to see the sights while gliding smoothly through the streets. Their Copenhagen Segway Tour is a favorite among tourists, offering an exciting way to explore the city's landmarks while covering more ground in less time. The tour lasts about 1.5 to 2 hours, and prices start at DKK 550 per person. It includes visits to popular sites like Tivoli Gardens, Rosenborg Castle, and the famous Nyhavn waterfront. Segway Tours Copenhagen also offers evening tours for a chance to see the city lit up under the evening sky, creating a truly magical experience. Segway Tours Copenhagen guarantees a memorable and enjoyable ride. For more information, check out their website at www.segway-tours.dk.

City Wonders: For history buffs and royal enthusiasts, City Wonders offers a selection of immersive tours focused on Copenhagen's royal heritage. Their Royal Copenhagen Tour is a highly recommended experience for those eager to dive deep into the city's monarchical past. This 3-hour tour, priced at around DKK 495, takes visitors through royal landmarks such as the Amalienborg Palace, the Marble Church, and Rosenborg Castle, providing detailed commentary about Denmark's royal family, their traditions, and the significance of these historic sites. City Wonders is known for offering small-group tours, ensuring a more intimate and personalized experience. Their knowledgeable guides bring the stories of the Danish monarchy to life, often sharing lesser-known facts and anecdotes that make the royal history come alive. With an emphasis on culture, history, and architecture, City Wonders provides a rich and educational experience for anyone interested in the city's royal heritage. Their website, www.citywonders.com, offers additional tour options and detailed booking information.

Copenhagen Free Walking Tours: For those on a budget or looking for a relaxed and flexible tour, Copenhagen Free Walking Tours offers an excellent way to discover the city without breaking the bank. This operator is unique in that they provide a pay-what-you-want model, allowing visitors to choose how much to tip at the end of the tour based on their experience. This makes it an accessible option for travelers of all budgets, while still ensuring high-quality service. Copenhagen Free Walking Tours offers a range of tours, including a general city walking tour and themed tours like the Copenhagen's Hidden Gems Tour and the Copenhagen Food Tour, which allows visitors to explore the city's culinary culture on foot. The general tour is approximately 2.5 hours long and covers must-see locations like City Hall Square, the historic canals, and the famous Little Mermaid statue, while the food tour dives into the city's vibrant food scene. The guides at Copenhagen Free Walking Tours are passionate about sharing the city's rich history and vibrant culture. They combine storytelling with local insights to offer a unique and engaging experience. Since the tours are conducted on foot, they allow for a more personal exploration of Copenhagen's charm, encouraging guests to ask questions and interact with the guides. For more details, visit www.copenhagenfreewalkingtours.dk.

CHAPTER 5
PRACTICAL INFORMATION AND GUIDANCE

5.1 Maps and Navigation

SCAN THE QR CODE WITH A DEVICE TO VIEW A COMPREHENSIVE AND LARGER MAP OF COPENHAGEN

Navigating a new city can sometimes feel daunting, but with the right tools, it can also become one of the most exciting parts of the journey. Copenhagen, Denmark's capital, is a city that is not only easy to explore but also rich in culture, history, and modernity. Whether you are strolling along the canals, cycling through the city, or visiting the many museums and parks, understanding how to access Copenhagen's maps—both digitally and through traditional means—can greatly enhance your travel experience.

The Copenhagen Tourist Map: For those who prefer the tactile experience of a paper map, Copenhagen offers a variety of printed tourist maps that you can pick up at key locations throughout the city. These maps are often available at tourist information centers, hotels, and major transportation hubs such as the Central Station or the airport. The Copenhagen Tourist Map is designed to help visitors navigate the city's main attractions, public transport routes, and neighborhoods with ease. Typically, these maps highlight key areas like the iconic Tivoli Gardens, Nyhavn, the historic center, and the city's many bike paths. In addition to pointing out major landmarks, these paper maps often include a helpful index, showing key streets, transportation lines, and public facilities such as restrooms and visitor centers. While the paper map may not offer real-time updates like a digital map, it remains a reliable tool for getting a sense of the city's layout and planning your day. The simplicity of unfolding a map, especially when walking through Copenhagen's charming streets, is an experience many travelers still cherish. If you're in need of a physical map, simply ask for one at the tourist offices or look for a kiosk in the central areas.

Digital Maps: In today's world, digital maps have become indispensable, especially when it comes to getting around a foreign city. Copenhagen offers multiple ways to access its map digitally, allowing for seamless navigation no matter where you are in the city. One of the most widely used apps is Google Maps, which provides comprehensive and up-to-date directions for walking, cycling, public transportation, and driving. The app also gives real-time data on delays or disruptions in public transport, making it an excellent tool for getting around efficiently. In addition to Google Maps, there are also specialized apps designed specifically for Copenhagen. The "Citymapper" app is an excellent choice for travelers looking to navigate the city's public transport system, as it provides detailed directions on buses, metro, and trains, alongside walking and cycling routes. Another popular app is "Copenhagen City Guide," which not only offers interactive maps but also provides insightful tips on local attractions, restaurants, and hidden gems within the city. Both of these apps can be easily downloaded and used offline, a handy feature if you're traveling without constant internet access. Moreover, the City of Copenhagen offers its own official digital map. Available on the city's official website, this interactive map provides a bird's-eye view of Copenhagen's districts, parks, museums, and other important landmarks. It also highlights bike lanes and pedestrian routes, which are especially useful in a city where cycling is a popular mode of transportation. The city's website offers a variety of tools and filters to help you find exactly what you're looking for, from the nearest metro station to the closest public restroom.

Offline Navigation: While digital maps are extremely useful, they are often reliant on a stable internet connection. If you prefer to explore Copenhagen without relying on a constant data connection, there are several ways to access offline maps. Many of the digital map apps mentioned earlier, such as Google Maps and Citymapper, allow you to download maps for offline use before you start your journey. This feature is particularly useful when you're out of Wi-Fi range or have limited data access while traveling. Additionally, printed versions of Copenhagen's city map are also an excellent offline option, ensuring that you can explore the city even in areas where your phone might not have a signal. Most maps you pick up will include details on how to use public transport, which can be crucial in understanding the layout of the city and planning your itinerary.

Comprehensive Maps: For a more detailed, in-depth map experience, visitors can access a comprehensive map of Copenhagen by using the QR code or link provided in this guide. By simply scanning the QR code with your smartphone, you will be directed to a fully interactive map that encompasses every corner of Copenhagen. This digital map not only includes locations of major tourist attractions but also offers detailed insights into lesser-known spots, hidden cafes, and peaceful parks, making it a perfect tool for any type of traveler. The interactive nature of this map allows you to zoom in and out, search for specific places, and receive detailed directions, helping you feel confident in your ability to explore Copenhagen at your own pace.

5.2 Four Days Itinerary

A well-planned itinerary is essential to make the most of your time in this charming city. With four days in Copenhagen, you will have just enough time to explore its iconic landmarks, enjoy its vibrant neighborhoods, and experience the lifestyle that makes this city so special.

Day One: Exploring the Heart of Copenhagen
Start your first day in Copenhagen by immersing yourself in the city's vibrant culture and history. Begin at Rådhuspladsen (City Hall Square), where you can admire the impressive architecture of the Copenhagen City Hall. From here, take a stroll down Strøget, one of Europe's longest pedestrian shopping streets. Strøget is a lively area filled with boutiques, department stores, cafes, and street performers. It's the perfect place to get a feel for the local atmosphere and perhaps pick up a few souvenirs. As you continue down Strøget, make your way to the famous Nyhavn district. Known for its colorful 17th-century townhouses, Nyhavn is the quintessential Copenhagen postcard. It is a beautiful place to wander, with its many cafes and restaurants lining the canal. You can choose to sit down for a leisurely lunch by the water and enjoy Danish specialties such as smørrebrød (open-faced sandwiches). After lunch, take a canal tour to see Copenhagen from a different perspective. The boat ride will take you past landmarks like the Opera House, Amalienborg Palace, and the Black Diamond Library. In the afternoon, visit the iconic Amalienborg Palace, the residence of the Danish royal family. Be sure to catch the Changing of the Guard ceremony, which takes place at noon, offering visitors a glimpse into the royal traditions. The palace is an elegant piece of history, and a visit to its museum provides insight into the royal family's way of life. Finish your first day by walking along the picturesque Christiansborg Palace, home to the Danish Parliament. Christiansborg offers fascinating tours, where you can explore its historic chambers and learn about the Danish political system. If you have the time, consider visiting the Tivoli Gardens, especially if your visit is in the evening. This historic amusement park offers a magical atmosphere with its bright lights, historic rides, and live performances.

Day Two: A Journey Through Copenhagen's Art and History
The second day of your itinerary is dedicated to the artistic and cultural treasures of Copenhagen. Start with a visit to the National Gallery of Denmark (Statens Museum for Kunst). The museum boasts an impressive collection of Danish and international art from the 14th century to the present day. From works by renowned Danish painters to modern art installations, the National Gallery is a paradise for art lovers. Afterward, head to the nearby Frederiksborg Castle in Hillerød, a bit outside the city center but easily accessible by train.

Frederiksborg Castle is one of Denmark's most stunning landmarks, built during the reign of King Christian IV. The castle houses the Museum of National History, where you can explore exhibits on Denmark's royal past, historical paintings, and artifacts. The stunning gardens surrounding the castle are perfect for a relaxing stroll, with their formal design and tranquil water features. Returning to Copenhagen in the afternoon, make your way to the Rosenborg Castle, another architectural gem in the city. This Renaissance castle is home to the Danish crown jewels, royal regalia, and royal collections. Walking through its lavish rooms and corridors will give you a sense of the grandeur of Denmark's monarchy. For dinner, head to the Meatpacking District (Kødbyen), an area known for its trendy restaurants and vibrant nightlife. Here, you can sample modern Danish cuisine in a relaxed setting, and perhaps even enjoy a drink at one of the district's lively bars.

Day Three: Copenhagen's Natural Beauty and Modern Attractions
On your third day in Copenhagen, take some time to enjoy the city's natural beauty and modern attractions. Begin by visiting the Botanical Gardens, one of the largest and most beautiful green spaces in Copenhagen. The gardens are home to a vast collection of plants from around the world, including exotic species in its impressive glasshouses. It's the perfect spot to enjoy a peaceful morning walk among the flora. Afterward, make your way to the modern and artistic district of Vesterbro. This area has evolved into one of the city's trendiest neighborhoods, with a growing number of cafes, galleries, and creative spaces. A visit to the Copenhagen Art Center is highly recommended if you're interested in contemporary art. As you explore Vesterbro, you'll also find a number of boutiques and design shops, ideal for picking up unique items. Next, head towards the district of Christianshavn, home to the architectural wonder of the Danish Architecture Center (DAC). Located on the waterfront, this space is dedicated to the best of Danish design and architecture. The center offers fascinating exhibits on sustainable building practices, urban development, and the history of Danish architecture. Afterward, take a walk around the famous Danish modernist landmark, the Copenhagen Opera House, which sits across the water from Amalienborg Palace. Later in the day, venture to the modern district of Ørestad. This area is an example of cutting-edge urban planning, with impressive contemporary buildings such as the iconic Cactus Tower and the Royal Arena. Ørestad is also home to the beautiful Islands Brygge promenade, where you can enjoy a walk along the water and relax at one of the many cafes. Finish the day with a trip to the Louisiana Museum of Modern Art, located just

outside Copenhagen. It offers an extraordinary collection of contemporary art, set against the backdrop of beautiful coastal views. The museum's sculpture park and exhibitions are a must-see for those with an interest in modern art and design.

Day Four: Copenhagen's Quirky Side and Local Delights
Your final day in Copenhagen will offer a chance to explore the city's quirkier side. Begin your day with a visit to the unique Freetown Christiania, an autonomous neighborhood that has developed its own rules and lifestyle. Christiania is a haven for artists, musicians, and free spirits, with vibrant murals, quirky shops, and communal living spaces. Take a leisurely walk through this fascinating area and embrace the eclectic atmosphere that defines it. Next, head to the Carlsberg Brewery, one of Copenhagen's most iconic landmarks. Take a tour of the brewery and learn about the history of Carlsberg, one of Denmark's most famous exports. The tour offers an informative and fun experience, and you'll be able to taste the various beers produced here. In the afternoon, visit the National Museum of Denmark, where you can learn about the country's rich cultural history. The museum houses fascinating exhibits on Danish archaeology, Viking history, and the country's cultural evolution. It's an ideal place to gain a deeper understanding of Denmark's heritage. For your last evening, explore the vibrant food scene of Copenhagen. Head to the Torvehallerne Market, where you can indulge in a variety of Danish delicacies, including fresh seafood, pastries, and gourmet street food. The market is a great place to sample the flavors of Copenhagen in a lively and casual setting.

5.3 Essential Packing List

Packing for a trip to Copenhagen can be a delightful yet challenging task, as the city's weather and culture demand certain considerations to ensure your visit is as enjoyable and comfortable as possible. Copenhagen, known for its trendy mix of modern design, historic charm, and picturesque waterways, offers visitors a wide variety of experiences. However, to make the most of your stay in Denmark's capital, it's important to pack thoughtfully, keeping in mind the city's unpredictable weather, biking culture, and vibrant urban life. Understanding the essentials of what to pack for Copenhagen will help ensure that you are well-prepared for your adventure, no matter the season

Weather-Appropriate Clothing: Copenhagen's weather can be highly variable, even within a single day, which makes it essential to pack clothing that allows you to adapt easily to changing conditions. During the summer months, from June to August, the weather can range from mild to warm, with daytime temperatures averaging between 15°C to 22°C (59°F to 72°F). However, evenings can still be chilly, so packing layers is a good strategy. A lightweight, breathable jacket or sweater can come in handy for evening strolls along the harbor or outdoor dinners in the city's trendy courtyards. Lightweight clothing like t-shirts, shorts, and sundresses are appropriate for the daytime, but it's wise to carry a rain jacket or windbreaker as Copenhagen is known for its occasional showers and breezy weather. The fall months, from September to November, bring cooler temperatures and more frequent rain showers, requiring slightly heavier clothing. A versatile jacket that is both warm and waterproof will serve you well, and layering is again key. Packing a scarf, gloves, and warm hats for colder evenings is highly recommended, particularly as the temperatures drop into single digits Celsius (around 40°F). In winter, from December to February, Copenhagen can be quite cold, with temperatures dipping below freezing, so a well-insulated, waterproof coat is crucial. Thermal undergarments, woolen socks, and sturdy shoes will keep you comfortable while you explore the wintery streets. Similarly, in spring, which can be quite unpredictable, layering remains important, with a good-quality raincoat, sturdy boots, and an umbrella being key components of your packing list.

Comfortable Footwear: Copenhagen is a very walkable city, with many attractions, shopping districts, and cafes situated within walking distance of each other. As such, packing comfortable footwear is a must. While the cobblestone streets and narrow alleys lend Copenhagen its old-world charm, they can be challenging to navigate with ill-fitting shoes. Walking shoes or sneakers with good arch support are recommended for long days of sightseeing. If you plan on biking—an integral part of Copenhagen's culture—consider packing shoes that can be easily worn with pedals or cycling-specific footwear. During the colder months, insulated and waterproof footwear becomes essential for keeping your feet warm and dry. A sturdy pair of boots with good traction will help you stay comfortable while walking through Copenhagen's often slippery streets in winter. For the summer months, breathable sandals or comfortable flats will suffice for casual outings, but if you plan to attend formal events, packing a pair of dressier shoes is a good idea.

Biking Gear: Copenhagen is one of the most bike-friendly cities in the world, with an extensive network of bike lanes and bike-sharing programs. If you plan to rent a bike during your stay, you may want to pack some additional gear to make your cycling experience more enjoyable. A comfortable backpack or crossbody bag is ideal for carrying your essentials while riding. If you have a helmet preference, consider bringing your own, though bikes rented in Copenhagen typically come with helmets as part of the rental service. In the summer months, it's a good idea to bring sunscreen to protect yourself from the sun while biking. Sunglasses, preferably polarized, are also a good addition for both sunny days and when cycling under cloudy skies, as they can reduce glare from the roads and waterways. Cycling gloves are another item to consider, especially if you plan to take long bike rides through the city or along Copenhagen's scenic harborfront paths.

Travel Essentials: In terms of travel documents and accessories, it's important to have all your necessary paperwork, such as your passport, any required visas, and hotel reservation details, easily accessible. A travel organizer or document holder can keep everything in one place. When traveling around Copenhagen, a local transportation card or pass—such as the City Pass or Rejsekort for trains and buses—will make it easier to get around without having to buy tickets for every journey. It's advisable to download the Citymapper app or have Google Maps ready on your smartphone for seamless navigation. Copenhagen has a strong culture of sustainability, and many locals prefer reusable items to minimize waste. A refillable water bottle is a great addition to your packing list, as tap water in Copenhagen is some of the cleanest in Europe. Carrying a compact reusable shopping bag for any purchases you make is also in line with the city's eco-friendly ethos. Since Copenhagen is a cashless society, most transactions are made via credit card, and many shops even offer the option to pay through Apple Pay or MobilePay, so it's important to carry your cards securely.

Toiletries and Personal Care Items: Copenhagen's standard of personal hygiene and wellness is high, and most hotels and accommodations will provide the basic toiletries. However, packing your own items ensures you have everything you need, especially for longer stays. Make sure to pack a good sunscreen, as the northern latitude of Denmark means that even during overcast days, UV rays can still be strong. A high-quality moisturizer is also recommended for both sun protection and wind protection, as Copenhagen's coastal climate can dry out skin. For winter travelers, a thick, nourishing lip balm and hand cream are essential items to prevent your skin from becoming cracked or dry in the cold wind. If you plan to visit spas or swim in Copenhagen's public pools, packing a swimsuit or swim trunks is a good idea, as well as a towel or robe, although many pools provide these items for you.

Electronics and Charging Equipment: In today's connected world, your smartphone is likely one of the most important tools you will need for your Copenhagen trip. Be sure to pack the necessary chargers for your phone, tablet, or laptop, and consider carrying a portable power bank to ensure that your devices remain powered during long days of exploring the city. Copenhagen also offers free Wi-Fi in many public spaces, including cafes and libraries, but having your own data plan or a local SIM card may help you stay connected during your stay. If you're an avid photographer, packing a lightweight camera or a smartphone with a high-quality camera is a great way to capture Copenhagen's beauty. A travel adapter will be essential for charging your devices, as Denmark uses the European standard of two-pronged plugs with 230V power.

5.4 Setting Your Travel Budget
Copenhagen can also be known for its relatively high cost of living. Whether you are a budget-conscious traveler or planning a luxury trip, understanding how to set a proper travel budget for Copenhagen is essential to ensure you make the most of your visit without overspending. Creating a comprehensive travel budget involves more than just figuring out your accommodation costs; it includes managing your expenses for food, transportation, sightseeing, and unexpected expenditures. To help guide you through this process, here are some essential tips for setting your travel budget when visiting Copenhagen.

Understanding Copenhagen's Cost of Living: Before you begin planning your budget, it's crucial to have a clear understanding of the cost of living in Copenhagen. As one of the more expensive cities in Europe, Copenhagen's prices can be daunting for first-time visitors, especially in areas such as dining, transportation, and accommodation. However, understanding this beforehand will allow you to make informed decisions about where and how you spend your money. In general, you will find that meals in Copenhagen can be pricey, especially in the city center and in tourist hotspots like Nyhavn or Tivoli Gardens. A simple meal at an inexpensive restaurant might cost between 100-150 DKK (Danish Kroner), while a three-course meal in a mid-range restaurant can easily set you back 300-600 DKK per person. On the other hand, if you're willing to eat at local cafes or visit food markets, you can find delicious and more affordable options. Copenhagen's public transportation system is also fairly easy to navigate, but it can add up if you're frequently moving between different parts of the city. To manage this, try researching the average costs for the types of activities you're interested in—whether you plan to explore museums, take boat tours, or visit parks. This will give you a clearer picture of how to allocate your funds for each aspect of the trip.

Prioritize Your Accommodation Choices: Accommodation is often the largest portion of a travel budget, and Copenhagen offers a wide range of options to suit different preferences and budgets. From luxury hotels to budget-friendly hostels and even Airbnb rentals, the city's diverse selection provides plenty of choices depending on your financial situation. If you are aiming for a more affordable stay, consider staying outside the city center or exploring options in the trendy Vesterbro or Nørrebro neighborhoods, which are often less expensive than the tourist-heavy areas around Nyhavn. Additionally, Copenhagen has an excellent network of hostels, where you can find comfortable and affordable rooms for a fraction of the price of hotels. Booking accommodation in advance can also help you find better deals, as last-minute bookings often come with a higher price tag. For those who are open to unique experiences, consider staying in a boutique guesthouse or a shared apartment. This not only offers an authentic, local experience but also helps you save money by cooking your own meals or sharing the cost of accommodation with other travelers. Be sure to research the location of your accommodation in relation to the city's attractions and transportation options. Staying near a metro station can save you both time and money in the long run.

Managing Your Food and Dining Expenses: One of the joys of visiting Copenhagen is the city's renowned culinary scene, with everything from Michelin-starred restaurants to food markets and casual eateries. However, dining out regularly in Copenhagen can quickly add up, especially if you stick to high-end restaurants. It is wise to plan your meals in advance to avoid unexpected costs. To manage food costs effectively, consider mixing high-end dining experiences with more affordable options. Copenhagen is famous for its street food markets, such as the Reffen Street Food Market in Refshaleøen and Torvehallerne Market, where you can sample a wide variety of delicious and reasonably priced local dishes. Opting for these food markets or smaller, local cafes allows you to experience authentic Danish cuisine without breaking your budget. If you are staying in an Airbnb or have access to a kitchen in your accommodation, it is a good idea to shop for groceries at one of Copenhagen's many local supermarkets like Føtex, Netto, or Lidl. Not only does this allow you to prepare your own meals, but it also gives you the flexibility to cook traditional Danish dishes like frikadeller (meatballs) or smørrebrød (open-faced sandwiches) without the added cost of eating out. Additionally, when dining out, be mindful of the service charge. In Denmark, tipping is not mandatory, and service charges are often included in the bill. If you receive exceptional service, however, you can round up the bill or leave a small tip as a gesture of appreciation.

Transportation: Copenhagen has a highly efficient public transportation system, including buses, trains, and the metro. While transportation is generally reliable and easy to use, the costs can add up if you're taking multiple trips throughout the day. Fortunately, there are several ways to manage your transportation expenses and make the most of the city's infrastructure. The best way to save on transportation is by purchasing a travel pass. The Copenhagen Card, for example, offers unlimited access to public transport as well as free admission to many of the city's top attractions, such as Tivoli Gardens, the National Museum of Denmark, and Rosenborg Castle. It can be purchased for 24, 48, 72, or 120 hours, and the more days you purchase, the better value you get. If you plan on visiting multiple attractions or will be traveling extensively within the city, the Copenhagen Card is a fantastic option to save both on transport and entry fees. Alternatively, if your travel needs are less intensive, you can buy individual tickets for the metro or buses. Copenhagen also offers a mobile app called "DOT Tickets," where you can purchase tickets for buses, trains, and the metro. This app is convenient for travelers who need to pay as they go or don't want to commit to a longer-term pass.

Budget for Unexpected Costs and Souvenirs: Even with a well-planned budget, it's important to set aside some money for unexpected expenses. These might include sudden taxi rides, unplanned shopping, or experiencing an impromptu activity that catches your eye. Copenhagen has plenty of hidden gems, from boutique shops to spontaneous live performances, and it's essential to be prepared for these moments. Setting aside a contingency fund—perhaps around 10-15% of your overall travel budget—will help ensure that you can enjoy these unexpected experiences without the stress of overspending. Additionally, while Copenhagen offers a range of experiences that are free or affordable, souvenirs and small purchases can accumulate over time. Whether you're picking up Danish design items, locally made products, or unique pieces of art, having a small allowance for souvenirs will ensure you leave with memories of your trip without compromising your overall budget.

5.5 Visa Requirements and Entry Procedures

When planning a trip to Copenhagen, it is essential to be aware of the visa requirements and entry procedures to ensure a smooth and hassle-free arrival. Copenhagen, as the capital of Denmark, is part of the Schengen Area, which includes several European countries. This means that travelers from most countries outside the Schengen Zone will need a visa for entry. However, the visa requirements can vary depending on the visitor's nationality and the purpose of the visit, whether for tourism, business, or other purposes.

Entry by Air Travel: Copenhagen's main gateway is the Copenhagen Airport (Kastrup), one of the busiest airports in Scandinavia, situated just 8 kilometers south of the city center. For travelers arriving by air, the entry process is quite straightforward, but it is important to ensure all the necessary documentation is in place before departure. Visitors from countries within the Schengen Area do not require any additional paperwork or visa for entry, as Denmark is part of this region. For travelers from outside the Schengen Area, a Schengen visa is required. This visa allows entry into Denmark as well as other countries in the Schengen Zone, provided the traveler does not exceed the allowed duration of stay. The Schengen visa generally allows a stay of up to 90 days within a 180-day period. It is advisable to apply for this visa well in advance of the trip, as processing times can vary depending on the applicant's nationality and the embassy or consulate they apply to. Upon arrival at Copenhagen Airport, non-EU travelers holding a Schengen visa will be directed to immigration counters where they must present their passport, visa, and any additional documents requested by the border officer. Commonly required documents include proof of accommodation, travel insurance, sufficient funds for the duration of the stay, and return flight tickets. The immigration process at Copenhagen Airport is efficient, but during peak times, it may take a little longer to clear customs.

Entry by Train: Copenhagen is well-connected to major European cities by train, making rail travel a popular choice for visitors arriving from nearby countries. The city is served by the Copenhagen Central Station, which is situated in the heart of the city and is easily accessible from all parts of Copenhagen. Visitors traveling by train from other Schengen countries do not need a visa, as they will be entering Denmark within the Schengen Area. For those arriving from non-Schengen countries, the entry requirements are similar to air travel. They will need to pass through immigration checks, where they will need to present their passport and any necessary documents. For travelers arriving by train from countries outside the Schengen Area, it is crucial to be aware of the specific entry requirements. Train services from countries such as Sweden and Germany pass through immigration and customs checks at the station. For instance, when traveling from Germany, the trains pass through a border checkpoint where travelers will be required to show their travel documents. Similar checks are conducted for trains coming from Sweden, although travel between these countries and Denmark is usually more seamless, particularly for passengers from Schengen Area nations. Trains offer a scenic and comfortable way to travel to Copenhagen, and the station itself is equipped with modern amenities such as restaurants, shops, and currency exchange services. For those arriving by train, it is always advisable to check the latest schedules and train requirements, as entry procedures can vary slightly depending on the train operator and the country of departure.

Entry by Road: For travelers entering Copenhagen by car, the entry procedure is similar to other modes of transportation. Denmark is well-linked to neighboring countries, including Sweden and Germany, by road. The E4 highway connects Copenhagen to Sweden, while the E47 and E55 highways provide direct routes from Germany. These highways are well-maintained, making it a convenient and efficient way to travel into the city. Travelers from other EU and Schengen countries entering Denmark by road do not need to stop at border control for passport checks, as Denmark is part of the Schengen Area. However, visitors from non-Schengen countries will still need to be prepared for customs checks. While there are no routine border control checks when entering Denmark by car, visitors arriving from outside the Schengen Zone may be required to show their passport and relevant documentation at any checkpoints along the way, especially if traveling from a non-Schengen country like Sweden or Germany. For those driving in Denmark, it is important to note the country's road regulations. Denmark has a strict zero-tolerance policy on drinking and driving, and drivers must always carry their driver's license, vehicle registration, and proof of insurance. It is also advisable to familiarize oneself with the Danish road signs, speed limits, and other traffic laws to ensure a safe and legal entry into Copenhagen.

Additional Considerations for Travelers to Copenhagen: Copenhagen is known for its easy access and efficiency when it comes to entry procedures, but visitors should remain vigilant about the latest travel advisories and changes to immigration rules. It is highly recommended to check the latest visa requirements, as these can occasionally change due to shifting political landscapes or changes in Denmark's immigration policies. It is also worth noting that Denmark has certain health and safety requirements for travelers. For instance, visitors from certain countries may be required to present a vaccination certificate upon arrival, particularly for diseases like yellow fever. Travelers should check with the Danish embassy or consulate in their home country for any health-related entry restrictions. Lastly, while Copenhagen is a welcoming city with a high level of English proficiency, it is always beneficial for visitors to familiarize themselves with some basic Danish phrases and cultural etiquette. Denmark has a rich history, and many visitors appreciate understanding a few words of the local language to enrich their travel experience.

5.6 Safety Tips and Emergency Contacts

Copenhagen, often regarded as one of the safest cities in Europe, is a welcoming destination for travelers, offering a vibrant cultural scene, picturesque landscapes, and an efficient public transport system. Despite its reputation for safety, like any major city, it is always wise for visitors to remain vigilant and prepared for any unforeseen circumstances. With its low crime rates, excellent healthcare services, and well-organized emergency response systems, Copenhagen provides a sense of security that allows travelers to focus on exploring the city. However, being aware of key safety tips and knowing how to handle emergencies is essential to ensure a smooth and enjoyable trip.

General Safety Tips for Visitors: Copenhagen is known for its relatively low crime rate, particularly when compared to other major cities around the world. Nevertheless, like in any large urban area, petty crimes such as pickpocketing can occasionally occur, particularly in crowded tourist areas like Nyhavn, Strøget, and Tivoli Gardens. To minimize the risk of falling victim to such crimes, it is advisable to keep your valuables secure and avoid displaying expensive items such as cameras, phones, and jewelry in crowded places. Use a cross-body bag or a money belt to keep your personal items close to you, and always be cautious when navigating busy areas. While violent crime is rare in Copenhagen, it is still important to exercise caution in unfamiliar neighborhoods after dark. Stick to well-lit and populated streets, and if you are unsure of your route, it is best to ask a local for guidance. The Copenhagen locals are friendly and helpful, and most people speak English fluently, so communication is rarely a barrier. As always, it is important to trust your instincts—if something feels off, it is best to remove yourself from the situation. For those who enjoy cycling through the city, Copenhagen's bike lanes are renowned for being safe and well-organized. However, cyclists should still exercise caution when navigating through intersections and crosswalks. Always ensure that you follow traffic rules and signals, and wear a helmet if you plan to cycle in the city. Despite being a cyclist-friendly city, accidents can still occur, so being aware of your surroundings is key.

Health and Medical Safety: Copenhagen boasts an excellent healthcare system, and in case of a medical emergency, you can be confident that the city's hospitals and clinics are equipped to provide immediate care. In Denmark, healthcare is primarily funded through taxes, and visitors are entitled to emergency medical treatment under specific circumstances. However, it is always advisable to have comprehensive travel insurance that covers medical expenses, including potential repatriation, to avoid any unexpected financial burdens. If you experience a medical emergency, it is important to know where the nearest hospital or medical center is located. The Rigshospitalet, located in the Frederiksberg area, is the largest and most well-known hospital in Copenhagen and provides emergency care for both locals and visitors. For less urgent medical concerns, you can visit one of the many local healthcare centers or pharmacies, where you will receive professional advice and over-the-counter medication. Pharmacies in Copenhagen, such as Apoteket, are easy to find and offer a wide range of health products. Pharmacists in Denmark are well-trained and can provide guidance on minor ailments, from common colds to skin irritations. Many pharmacies also offer travel health services, including vaccinations for travelers heading to other parts of the world. If you need to contact a doctor urgently, the phone number to call is 1813, which is the national medical helpline. The service operates 24/7 and can direct you to the nearest hospital, clinic, or pharmacy based on your medical needs.

Emergency Services and Contact Information: In Copenhagen, emergency services are prompt and efficient, and it is essential to be aware of the contact information for various emergency situations. The general emergency number for police, fire, and ambulance services in Denmark is 112. This number is free of charge and will connect you to the appropriate emergency service, regardless of whether you are seeking assistance for a medical emergency, a fire, or a criminal incident. The call will be answered in Danish, but the operators are trained to speak English, so you will be able to communicate your needs effectively. For non-emergency police matters, such as reporting a lost passport or theft, you can contact the local police station directly. The Copenhagen Police, located in the Vesterbro district, can be reached at +45 35 66 14 48 for non-urgent situations. For more specific assistance, such as lost property or damage to personal belongings, local police will guide you through the necessary steps. Fire safety is also a priority in Copenhagen, and the city is well-prepared for emergencies. The Copenhagen Fire Department operates efficiently, with teams located throughout the city to handle fires, hazardous material incidents, and other emergencies. The fire department can be contacted through the same emergency number, 112, and they will quickly respond to any fire-related issues.

Safety for Solo Travelers: Copenhagen is known for being a safe city, even for solo travelers. Many people choose Copenhagen for solo trips because of its friendly and open atmosphere, and the city's low crime rate makes it an ideal destination for those exploring on their own. That said, it is always important to exercise common sense when traveling alone. If you're out late at night, try to stick to populated areas, and avoid wandering through isolated streets or neighborhoods. Solo travelers should also make use of the city's excellent public transportation system, which is not only reliable but also very safe. The metro system in Copenhagen operates around the clock on weekends, offering a convenient and secure way to travel around the city. Taxis are also readily available, but it's advisable to book them through an official app or phone number to ensure you're using a reputable service. Copenhagen's extensive cycling infrastructure also allows solo travelers to explore the city at their own pace, but again, it's essential to be aware of the traffic and adhere to safety regulations.

Personal Security for Tourists: Personal safety in Copenhagen is rarely a concern for tourists, but being aware of potential risks can help you make smarter decisions during your visit. As mentioned earlier, petty crimes like pickpocketing can occur in crowded tourist hotspots. To mitigate this risk, always keep your personal items secure and avoid carrying large amounts of cash. Using a money belt or a secure bag with anti-theft features is a good precautionary measure. Another safety consideration for tourists is to be cautious when accepting offers from street vendors or engaging with individuals offering unsolicited assistance. While most people in Copenhagen are friendly and approachable, it's wise to exercise caution and avoid situations that feel uncomfortable or potentially exploitative.

5.7 Currency Exchange and Banking Services

When visiting Copenhagen, understanding the local currency, banking services, and money matters is crucial to ensuring a smooth and enjoyable experience. Copenhagen is a modern, cosmopolitan city where various payment methods are accepted, from cash to cards, but knowing how to handle your finances in this Scandinavian hub will save you time and hassle during your stay. The official currency in Copenhagen is the Danish Krone (DKK), abbreviated as kr. It's important to note that while credit and debit cards are widely accepted throughout the city, especially in tourist areas, having some local currency on hand can be useful for smaller purchases, tips, or places that may not accept cards. Fortunately, exchanging currency, withdrawing cash, and accessing banking services are all relatively simple, thanks to Copenhagen's highly efficient banking system.

Currency Exchange and Bureau de Change Services in Copenhagen
Currency exchange in Copenhagen is straightforward, with multiple options available for exchanging foreign currency into Danish Krone. Bureau de change facilities can be found at key locations around the city, including major transport hubs, shopping centers, and tourist districts. If you're arriving by plane, you'll find currency exchange counters at Copenhagen Airport, which offer competitive rates for exchanging cash. However, it's always recommended to check the rates beforehand to avoid unfavorable conditions. Beyond the airport, one of the best places to exchange money is in the city center, particularly in areas where many tourists visit. Strøget, the city's main pedestrian shopping street, has several exchange services that allow you to switch your money into Danish Krone. These services usually accept a wide range of international currencies and offer a mix of cash exchange and prepaid travel cards. There are also ATMs throughout Copenhagen where you can withdraw Danish Krone directly from your international bank accounts. Be sure to inform your bank of your travel plans to avoid any issues with your cards, and check for any foreign

transaction fees that may apply. Some ATMs may charge withdrawal fees, so it's important to check the terms and conditions of the ATM operator before proceeding.

Using Credit and Debit Cards in Copenhagen: Copenhagen is known for its high level of digitalization, and card payments are the norm across most businesses. Visa, MasterCard, and American Express are widely accepted in restaurants, hotels, stores, and even in public transportation. Contactless payments are common, and you can easily tap your card to make purchases at most places, which is both convenient and secure. Additionally, the mobile payment system MobilePay has become incredibly popular in Denmark. This Danish payment app allows users to transfer money directly from their bank accounts via their smartphones. As a tourist, you may not have the app, but you'll find that most Danes use MobilePay to settle their bills quickly. It's important to note that tipping is not compulsory in Denmark, as service charges are included in the price, but small tips are appreciated for excellent service.

Banking in Copenhagen
Copenhagen is home to several major banks that offer services to both locals and international visitors. These banks provide a wide range of products and services, from currency exchange and savings accounts to investment options. While many visitors may not need a local bank account, it's useful to know where to go for banking services, particularly if you need cash, financial advice, or are dealing with larger transactions.

Danske Bank: Danske Bank, one of the largest financial institutions in Denmark, offers a broad array of services to visitors, including currency exchange and easy access to ATMs throughout Copenhagen. Located centrally, Danske Bank branches provide English-speaking staff, making it easy for tourists to navigate banking services. The branch at Amagertorv 1, located in the heart of Copenhagen's shopping district, is a prime spot for those in need of currency exchange services or general banking assistance.

Nordea: Another significant bank is Nordea, which also offers banking services tailored to international customers. Nordea operates multiple branches throughout Copenhagen, including one at Rådhuspladsen 61, right by City Hall. They provide a range of services for travelers, including access to international wire transfers, travel insurance, and currency exchange.

Jyske Bank: Jyske Bank is another popular choice among travelers looking for banking services in Copenhagen. Known for its customer-oriented approach, Jyske Bank offers currency exchange and a range of other banking products. The branch at Vesterbrogade 9 is centrally located and offers English-speaking staff to assist with international money transfers and account-related services. Jyske Bank is also known for its modern and user-friendly approach to banking, including online and mobile banking services that cater to both residents and visitors.

Saxo Bank: If you are looking for a more boutique experience, Saxo Bank offers a personalized approach to banking. While Saxo is best known for its online trading platform, the bank also has a presence in Copenhagen, offering investment advice and services. The branch at Rådhusstræde 16 specializes in wealth management and financial advisory services. Although it may not be the first choice for day-to-day banking, Saxo Bank is ideal for visitors who are looking for personalized investment advice or currency exchange services.

Spar Nord: Finally, there's Spar Nord, a bank that provides basic banking services with a local touch. They offer competitive rates for currency exchange and are known for their friendly customer service. The Spar Nord branch at Frederiksberggade 10 is easily accessible and offers English-speaking staff for those seeking assistance with international banking matters.

Managing Your Money

ATMs are plentiful throughout Copenhagen, and they are an efficient way to withdraw Danish Krone directly from your international bank account. Many banks in Copenhagen have partnerships with international ATM networks, making it easy to access cash with a foreign debit or credit card. Look for machines that belong to the Visa or MasterCard networks for the best exchange rates. It's important to note that some ATMs in Copenhagen may charge a fee for international withdrawals, so it's advisable to check your bank's policies regarding foreign ATM transactions before arriving. Many of the larger banks also offer international wire transfer services if you need to move larger sums of money from your home country. Additionally, some ATMs may offer the option to withdraw both small and large amounts of cash, depending on your needs.

5.8 Language, Communication and Useful Phrases

Danish is a North Germanic language, closely related to Swedish and Norwegian, but it is unique in its pronunciation and some aspects of grammar. Although Danish may seem challenging at first glance, especially with its distinct vowel sounds and soft consonants, you will quickly realize that most locals speak English fluently. Danish is taught from an early age in schools, and as a result, nearly 90% of the population can communicate in English to varying degrees. This linguistic skill is most prevalent in Copenhagen, where the majority of people working in tourism, hospitality, and retail are well-versed in English. However, as a traveler, learning a few basic phrases in Danish can go a long way in creating a connection with the locals and showing respect for their culture. Even though most people will respond to you in English, Danes appreciate when visitors make an effort to speak their language, and it can make your interactions more pleasant and personal.

Communication and Etiquette in Copenhagen: In Copenhagen, the communication style tends to be direct, clear, and respectful. Danes are known for their straightforwardness, but this should not be mistaken for rudeness. Their approach to communication is often open and honest, which contributes to a sense of equality and transparency in everyday life. This attitude extends to interactions with foreigners, and most people are willing to help you if you need directions or assistance. When greeting people, a handshake is the most common form of introduction, although in more casual settings, a friendly "hej" (pronounced "hi") is appropriate. It's also customary to address people by their first names, and in Copenhagen, personal space is valued, so it's best to avoid being overly touchy or overly familiar with strangers. As with any destination, understanding the basics of polite conversation can also help ease your way through any interactions. Saying "tak" (thank you) and "venligst" (please) are simple yet effective ways to show appreciation and respect. When addressing someone, using the formal "De" instead of the informal "du" may be appreciated, particularly in more formal settings. However, in general, Danish people are very laid-back and forgiving when it comes to language use, so don't be discouraged if you make a mistake.

Useful Phrases for Visiting Copenhagen
While you will certainly be able to get by in Copenhagen using English, knowing a few common Danish phrases will make your visit more enjoyable. Here are some key phrases to remember:

- "Hej" (hi) – This is a friendly and informal greeting commonly used in Copenhagen. It's an easy way to start a conversation with someone.
- "Hvordan har du det?" (How are you?) – A polite and friendly way to check in on someone's well-being.
- "Undskyld, kan du hjælpe mig?" (Excuse me, can you help me?) – A useful phrase when you're seeking assistance or directions.
- "Hvor er ...?" (Where is ...?) – Handy when trying to find specific locations, such as a museum, restaurant, or metro station.
- "Hvad koster det?" (How much does it cost?) – If you're shopping, this is an essential phrase to ask about the price of an item.
- "Jeg taler ikke dansk" (I don't speak Danish) – While many people will speak English, it's polite to let them know that you may not be fluent in Danish.
- "Tak" (Thank you) – A simple but essential word to express gratitude.
- "Skål" (Cheers) – This is a Danish toast, perfect for enjoying a drink with new friends or locals.

English in Copenhagen: As mentioned earlier, English is widely spoken in Copenhagen, especially among younger generations and those involved in the service and hospitality industries. Signs, menus, and information in public places such as museums, transport stations, and tourist attractions are typically available in both Danish and English. This makes Copenhagen an incredibly easy city to navigate for English-speaking travelers. However, it's worth noting that the level of English proficiency can vary depending on the area you are visiting. In more touristy districts, such as Nyhavn or the central parts of the city, English speakers will be abundant, and you'll have no problem communicating. In contrast, if you venture into more residential or less tourist-oriented neighborhoods, you may encounter fewer people who speak English. Nonetheless, even in these areas, locals will likely make an effort to help you, and simple gestures, such as pointing or using translation apps, can assist you in overcoming any communication gaps.

5.9 Shopping in Copenhagen

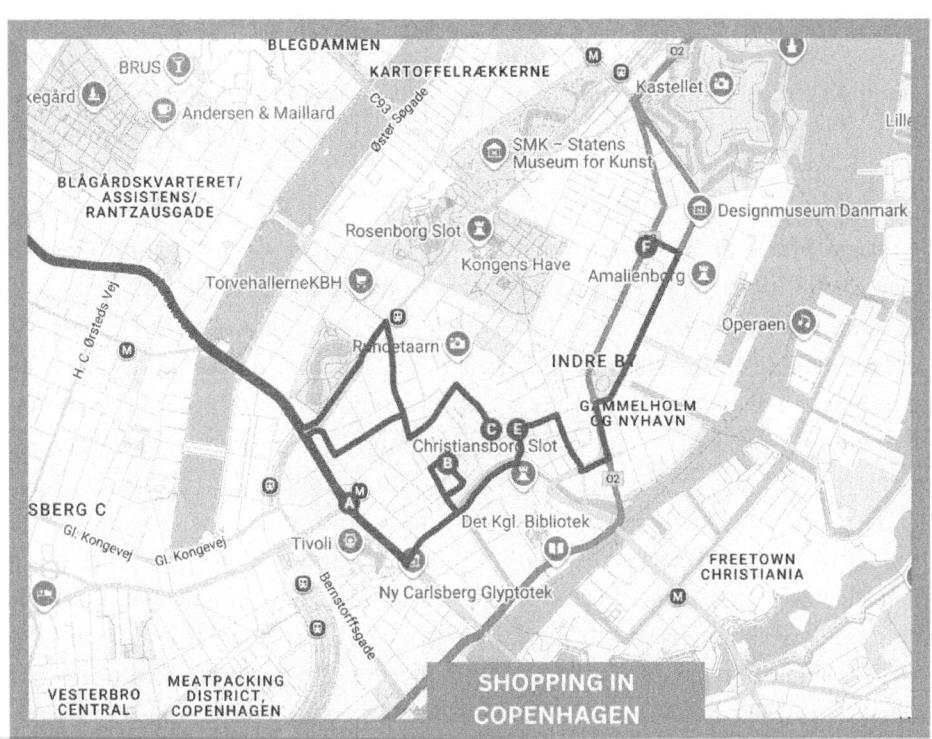

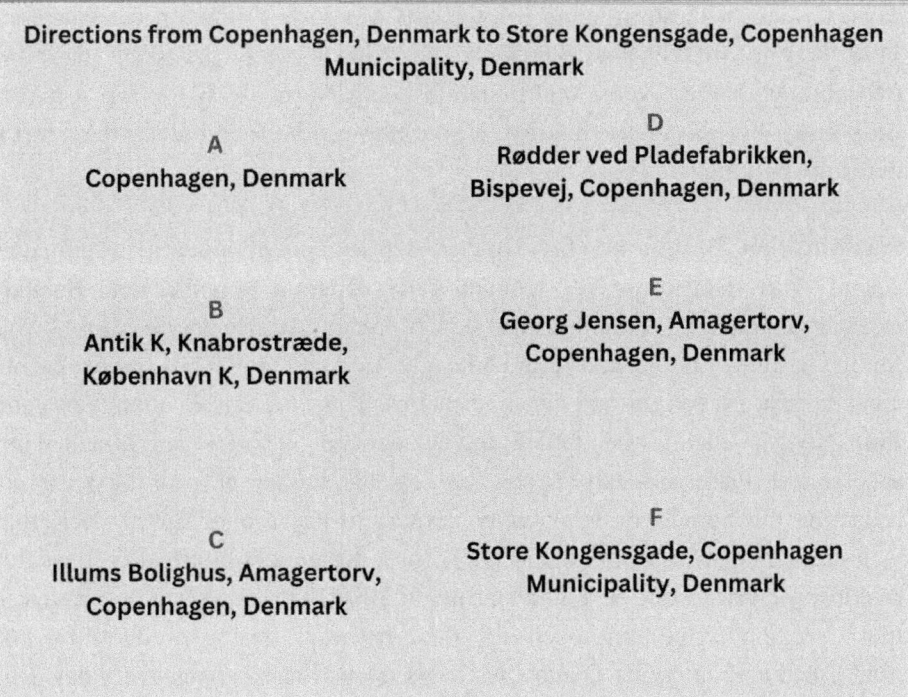

Directions from Copenhagen, Denmark to Store Kongensgade, Copenhagen Municipality, Denmark

A
Copenhagen, Denmark

B
Antik K, Knabrostræde, København K, Denmark

C
Illums Bolighus, Amagertorv, Copenhagen, Denmark

D
Rødder ved Pladefabrikken, Bispevej, Copenhagen, Denmark

E
Georg Jensen, Amagertorv, Copenhagen, Denmark

F
Store Kongensgade, Copenhagen Municipality, Denmark

Copenhagen is a treasure trove of shopping opportunities, offering everything from high-end boutiques to charming antique stores. Whether you're looking for high fashion, unique souvenirs, or vintage treasures, Copenhagen's diverse shopping scene promises something for every taste and budget. Here's a closer look at five exceptional shopping destinations in the city, each with its own unique offerings, ambiance, and charm.

Vintage Finds at Antik K: For those who love uncovering treasures from the past, Antik K offers an enchanting shopping experience. Nestled in the heart of Copenhagen's antique district, located on Kronprinsensgade, this store is a dream come true for antique enthusiasts. Specializing in vintage furniture, art, and decorative items, Antik K is filled with unique pieces from different eras, including mid-century modern designs, 19th-century Danish furniture, and classic Scandinavian glassware. In addition to furniture, the store also offers a variety of vintage jewelry, porcelain, and collectibles, with many items reflecting the craftsmanship and elegance of times gone by. Prices vary significantly depending on the item's rarity and age. Smaller trinkets like antique porcelain cups or vintage jewelry may cost anywhere from 300 to 1,500 DKK, while larger pieces such as a well-preserved cabinet or chandelier could set you back by 5,000 DKK to 20,000 DKK or more. Antik K is open seven days a week, with store hours from 10:00 AM to 6:00 PM on weekdays and 11:00 AM to 4:00 PM on Sundays. The store is easily accessible by public transport, with the nearest metro station being Nørreport Station, just a short walk away. For those traveling by car, parking can be found along the street or in nearby parking garages.

Scandinavian Design at Hay House: A true icon of modern Scandinavian design, Hay House on St. Kongensgade offers a sophisticated shopping experience that merges minimalist style with functional design. Hay is renowned for its furniture, home decor, and lifestyle products that focus on sleek lines, contemporary materials, and clean aesthetics. The store carries a range of items, from stylish chairs and tables to eye-catching textiles and small home accessories. Prices at Hay House are on the higher end of the spectrum, reflecting the brand's design quality. Expect to pay around 2,000 DKK for a well-crafted chair or up to 10,000 DKK for a designer sofa. Smaller items, like cushions or vases, can be found starting at 200 DKK. The store is a haven for those seeking a modern touch for their homes, offering products by both established and emerging Danish designers. Hay House is open every day, from

10:00 AM to 6:00 PM Monday through Saturday, and from 11:00 AM to 5:00 PM on Sundays. It's located within walking distance of Nyhavn, one of Copenhagen's most picturesque areas, and can be easily reached by public transport, including the Metro or Bus 1A, with a stop at Kongens Nytorv.

Designer Fashion at Illums Bolighus: For those looking to indulge in high-end design and luxury fashion, Illums Bolighus is the ultimate shopping destination. Situated at Amagertorv, right in the heart of Copenhagen's iconic shopping district, this department store offers an extensive selection of contemporary furniture, design objects, and fashion from leading international brands. The store combines Danish and international luxury brands, offering everything from elegant homeware to chic clothing. At Illums Bolighus, visitors will find upscale fashion labels like Chloé, Gucci, and Saint Laurent, as well as exclusive home furnishings and décor pieces. The prices here can be steep, with clothing items typically ranging from 1,000 DKK to 10,000 DKK, depending on the brand. Luxury furniture and decor can cost anywhere from 5,000 DKK for smaller items to 50,000 DKK for designer couches or tables. The store is open every day, from 10:00 AM to 6:00 PM, and offers extended hours on Fridays, staying open until 7:00 PM. It is centrally located, easily accessible by foot from the Strøget shopping street, Copenhagen's main pedestrian zone. For those using public transport, the Metro and several bus routes stop at Kongens Nytorv nearby.

Vintage and Retro Styles at Rødder: For a more eclectic shopping experience, Rødder is a must-visit. Located in the vibrant Vesterbro district, this boutique store is known for its curated collection of vintage and retro clothing, accessories, and home decor. The shop specializes in 20th-century fashion, with a strong focus on 1960s to 1980s styles, offering both men's and women's clothing. In addition to clothing, Rødder carries an impressive selection of vintage vinyl records, old-school cameras, and mid-century modern furniture. Prices at Rødder are more affordable than some of the city's high-end stores, with vintage T-shirts and jackets typically priced between 200 and 800 DKK. Designer items or rare vintage pieces can go up to 2,500 DKK. The store is a great option for travelers looking for unique souvenirs or one-of-a-kind fashion pieces that reflect Copenhagen's retro vibe. Rødder operates with slightly shorter hours, opening from 12:00 PM to 6:00 PM on weekdays and 11:00 AM to 4:00 PM on Saturdays. It is closed on Sundays. The store is easily reached via the Vesterport Station, which is a short walk away.

Artisan Craft and Jewelry at Georg Jensen: Finally, Georg Jensen, located at Strandvejen, is a landmark in Danish design, specializing in luxury silverware, jewelry, and home accessories. Founded in 1904, Georg Jensen is a true symbol of craftsmanship, offering elegant products that reflect Denmark's rich design heritage. Whether you're looking for a beautiful silver bracelet, a fine porcelain teapot, or a striking home decor item, Georg Jensen's store in Copenhagen is the place to find exquisite pieces that combine modern design with traditional techniques. Jewelry at Georg Jensen ranges from 1,000 DKK for simpler pieces to 20,000 DKK or more for intricate silver and diamond designs. The store also offers high-end silverware and luxury items for the home, with prices starting at around 500 DKK for smaller items, like trays or candles, and going up to several thousand Danish kroner for larger pieces. Georg Jensen's Copenhagen store operates from 10:00 AM to 6:00 PM, Monday through Saturday, and is closed on Sundays. The store is conveniently located near Amalienborg Palace, making it easy to incorporate a visit while exploring other historic landmarks in the city. Public transportation options, including buses and the Metro, make it simple to reach the store from various parts of Copenhagen.

5.10 Health and Wellness Centers

Copenhagen also excels in providing a variety of health and wellness services for visitors looking to recharge and refresh during their time in the city. Whether you are seeking to unwind with a luxurious spa experience, embark on a journey of holistic healing, or engage in fitness activities that refresh both the body and mind, Copenhagen offers a wide array of health and wellness centers that cater to all needs. The city's wellness offerings seamlessly blend relaxation, rejuvenation, and fitness, making it an ideal destination for travelers looking to prioritize their well-being.

A Visit to the Unique Fitness World Copenhagen: For those visitors who want to maintain their fitness routine while in Copenhagen, Fitness World is one of the most popular and comprehensive fitness centers in the city. Located in multiple spots throughout the city, Fitness World offers an extensive range of services, from state-of-the-art gym equipment to group classes such as yoga, Pilates, and spinning. These modern facilities also cater to tourists by offering short-term memberships, making it convenient for visitors who prefer a flexible approach to their fitness while traveling. Beyond the traditional gym experience, Fitness World also offers wellness features such as saunas, steam rooms, and even massage services, creating a holistic experience for those in need of relaxation after an intense workout. The ambiance within the facilities is one of openness and modernity, making it not only a place to work out but also a space for visitors to unwind and focus on their personal health goals. Whether you're someone who prefers cardio, strength training, or mindfulness exercises, Fitness World provides the perfect environment to maintain both your physical and mental health while in Copenhagen.

The Exclusive Water Wellness Experience at AquaSpa: AquaSpa, a renowned wellness center in Copenhagen, is the perfect sanctuary for those seeking a more luxurious and soothing experience. Specializing in water-based therapies, AquaSpa offers a range of treatments designed to detoxify, relax, and rejuvenate the body. The spa combines a variety of water-related wellness techniques, including hydrotherapy, saltwater pools, and steam rooms, all set within a serene and elegantly designed space. Visitors can indulge in a range of treatments, from deep tissue massages to facials and body scrubs, each of which uses high-quality, natural products sourced from around the world. AquaSpa also offers special packages that include access to its thermal experiences and private sauna rooms, where guests can unwind in a calm and quiet environment. Whether you're recovering from a long flight or simply seeking a break from the hustle and bustle of city life, AquaSpa provides an intimate and indulgent experience that will leave you feeling completely rejuvenated.

Holistic Health at The Wellness Lab Copenhagen: For those interested in a more holistic approach to health and wellness, The Wellness Lab Copenhagen offers personalized treatments and therapies that focus on both mind and body. Located in the heart of the city, The Wellness Lab focuses on fostering overall well-being through a combination of nutritional counseling, physical therapy, and mindfulness practices. One of the key highlights of this wellness center is its emphasis on stress reduction and mental clarity, providing guests with the tools to cultivate a calm and balanced lifestyle. Through services like personalized nutrition plans, yoga, meditation, and therapeutic massage, The Wellness Lab addresses the individual needs of each client, making it an ideal choice for visitors looking to improve their mental, physical, and emotional health. The center also offers workshops on various wellness topics, such as mindfulness, healthy living, and the importance of a balanced diet. For travelers who want to integrate a sense of well-being into their trip, The Wellness Lab is the ideal destination to reset and refresh.

Rejuvenation and Healing at Børsen Spa: Located in one of Copenhagen's most exclusive and historically significant buildings, Børsen Spa is a place where luxury and health meet. The spa's design draws inspiration from the classical beauty of Danish architecture while incorporating modern wellness treatments to create a harmonious environment. Børsen Spa's offerings range from indulgent massages to more specialized healing therapies such as acupuncture, reiki, and reflexology. The spa focuses on restoring the body's natural balance by combining Eastern and Western healing philosophies. Visitors can enjoy everything from soothing body scrubs to deeply relaxing aromatherapy massages. The luxurious atmosphere of Børsen Spa makes it a favorite among travelers looking for an upscale wellness experience that offers complete privacy and relaxation. This wellness center is also well known for its wellness retreats, which often include yoga sessions and detox programs designed to help guests cleanse both physically and mentally.

The Tranquil Sanctuary of Copenhagen's Vesterbro Wellness Center: For those who are seeking a peaceful retreat from the vibrant city life, the Vesterbro Wellness Center offers a serene environment for self-care and rejuvenation. Located in the trendy Vesterbro district, this wellness center has earned a reputation for its tranquil atmosphere and range of services designed to promote relaxation and mental clarity. The center specializes in providing therapeutic treatments, such as massages, acupuncture, and facials, all tailored to the individual needs of its clients. Vesterbro Wellness Center is an excellent destination for visitors looking to experience relaxation in a quiet, low-key setting. The center offers packages that cater to visitors who wish to indulge in a full day of wellness, combining massages with facial treatments, body wraps, and sauna experiences. Whether you seek an escape from the daily grind or need a restorative experience after a long journey, Vesterbro Wellness Center provides an intimate environment that promotes holistic well-being.

5.11 Useful Websites, Mobile Apps and Online Resources

In today's digital age, accessing information through websites, mobile apps, and online resources has become an integral part of traveling. For visitors to Copenhagen, these platforms serve as indispensable tools for navigating the city, finding things to do, understanding local culture, and getting real-time updates on transportation. Whether you're interested in booking tours, discovering hidden gems, or simply getting around the city with ease, there are a variety of websites and apps available that can enhance the Copenhagen experience. From planning your itinerary to navigating local transport, here's a deep dive into five must-have online resources for anyone visiting Copenhagen.

Visit Copenhagen: One of the most essential online resources for tourists heading to Copenhagen is the official Visit Copenhagen website. This comprehensive platform offers a wealth of information about the city's attractions, events, dining options, and accommodations. The website provides detailed listings on the most popular tourist destinations, including Tivoli Gardens, Nyhavn, and The Little Mermaid, as well as suggestions for lesser-known, off-the-beaten-path gems. In addition to being a hub for general travel information, Visit Copenhagen is tailored to help visitors create personalized itineraries. The site features easy-to-navigate filters that allow users to search for activities based on their interests—whether it's art, food, history, or outdoor adventures. The website also includes a calendar of events, so visitors can stay up-to-date on festivals, concerts, exhibitions, and seasonal activities happening throughout the year. Additionally, it offers resources like downloadable city maps, transportation guides, and suggested day trips to nearby areas. It's a fantastic starting point for anyone looking to get acquainted with Copenhagen before arriving, as it brings together everything a traveler needs to know in one convenient location.

Citymapper: Navigating Copenhagen's public transport system can be an enjoyable and efficient experience, thanks to apps like Citymapper, which is widely regarded as one of the best apps for urban transport. Whether you're taking the metro, bus, or a bike, Citymapper provides detailed information on the fastest routes, schedules, and real-time updates, ensuring visitors can get around the city with ease. The app also covers Copenhagen's boat services and provides walking directions for those who prefer to explore on foot. What sets Citymapper apart is its multi-modal trip planning feature, which allows users to choose from a variety of transport options—whether it's public transport, biking, or even car-sharing. The app calculates the most efficient routes based on current traffic conditions and public transport schedules, making it an indispensable tool for navigating the city. For visitors, this means no more guessing or getting lost in the city, as Citymapper provides clear, step-by-step guidance and real-time data on public transportation. It's available for both iOS and Android, and it also supports offline maps, which is particularly useful for tourists without access to mobile data.

Copenhagen Card: For visitors planning to explore Copenhagen's wide range of attractions, the Copenhagen Card app is a must-have. This digital card allows users to gain free access to more than 80 top attractions, including The National Museum of Denmark, The Danish Museum of Art & Design, and Christiansborg Palace, as well as free transport on buses, trains, and the metro. The app allows users to track the remaining validity of their card and offers easy access to discounts for several restaurants and shops. In addition to being a convenient tool for getting around, the Copenhagen Card app also helps visitors save time by skipping lines at many popular attractions. The app's built-in map and route planner further enhance its usefulness, directing cardholders to nearby attractions, restaurants, and transport options. Available for both iOS and Android devices, the Copenhagen Card app offers a streamlined way to enjoy the best of Copenhagen while saving money and time. Visitors can purchase and activate their card directly through the app, making it easy to start enjoying Copenhagen as soon as they arrive.

Yelp: When it comes to finding dining options and local experiences, Yelp is an essential app for anyone visiting Copenhagen. With a vast database of restaurants, bars, cafes, and even shops, Yelp allows visitors to explore the city's culinary scene through reviews and recommendations from both locals and fellow travelers. The app offers detailed information about each establishment, including opening hours, menus, customer ratings, and photos. What makes Yelp particularly valuable in Copenhagen is the user-generated content, which provides authentic insights into the best places to eat, drink, and shop in different neighborhoods of the city. Whether you're looking for a cozy café in Vesterbro, a fine-dining experience in Nyhavn, or the best street food in Nørrebro, Yelp helps you find exactly what you're looking for. The app also allows for easy reservation management and offers the ability to filter by location, price range, cuisine type, and even special features like vegetarian or vegan-friendly options. Yelp is available for both iOS and Android devices and is an essential app for foodies and explorers alike.

5.12 Internet Access and Connectivity

Having reliable internet access and connectivity is an essential aspect of any travel experience. Whether you're navigating the city's attractions, keeping in touch with loved ones, or simply researching your next destination, staying connected in Copenhagen is both straightforward and convenient. The city boasts an advanced digital infrastructure, making it easy for visitors to access the internet through various means. From free public Wi-Fi hotspots to local SIM cards and mobile hotspots, Copenhagen offers a range of options to meet the connectivity needs of all travelers. Understanding these options will help you make informed decisions about staying online during your visit.

Free Public Wi-Fi Hotspots Across Copenhagen: Copenhagen is a city that embraces digital connectivity, and one of the most convenient ways for visitors to stay connected is by taking advantage of the city's widespread public Wi-Fi. Various locations around the city, including parks, museums, libraries, and popular tourist sites, offer free Wi-Fi access. The Copenhagen City Library (Kulturhuset) and certain areas near major squares, such as Rådhuspladsen and Kongens Nytorv, provide visitors with the chance to surf the web, check emails, or use maps without having to rely on mobile data. Additionally, many cafes, restaurants, and even public transport services like the Metro provide free internet, ensuring you can stay connected while enjoying your day in the city. This widespread availability of free Wi-Fi helps visitors navigate Copenhagen seamlessly, especially if you need quick access to information on the go. However, it is important to be mindful of security when using public Wi-Fi networks, as they may not always be encrypted. Travelers should consider using a virtual private network (VPN) to safeguard their personal information while connected to these networks.

Renting a Mobile Hotspot for Flexible Connectivity: For those who prefer the convenience of having their own internet connection while exploring Copenhagen, renting a mobile hotspot is a great solution. Many rental services throughout the city offer portable Wi-Fi hotspots, providing unlimited data usage for travelers. These devices are lightweight, easy to carry, and can be used to connect multiple devices, such as smartphones, tablets, and laptops, simultaneously. This option is particularly useful for groups of travelers who want to stay connected without relying on public Wi-Fi. Mobile hotspot rentals are available at various locations in the city, including the airport, central train stations, and dedicated kiosks in popular tourist areas. You can also arrange to have the device delivered to your hotel or pick it up upon arrival in Copenhagen. This option provides reliable and fast internet access, ensuring that you can stay online no matter where you are in the city, whether you're at a cafe in Vesterbro, visiting a museum in the city center, or exploring Copenhagen's beautiful parks.

Local SIM Cards for Affordable Internet Access: For visitors planning to stay in Copenhagen for an extended period or those looking for a more permanent solution, purchasing a local SIM card is an excellent way to maintain connectivity. Denmark has several mobile network providers, including TDC, Telia, and 3, all of which offer prepaid SIM cards that cater to tourists. These SIM cards come with various data plans, allowing visitors to choose a package that suits their usage needs, whether for light browsing or more data-intensive activities like streaming videos or using GPS navigation. SIM cards can be purchased at kiosks, mobile phone shops, and even at Copenhagen Airport upon arrival. They are often sold with flexible data plans that include internet access, local calls, and international text messages. The process is straightforward, and the cards are usually compatible with most unlocked smartphones. Visitors should ensure their phones are unlocked before purchasing a SIM card. Having a local SIM card also allows you to avoid international roaming charges, providing a cost-effective solution to staying connected throughout your stay in Copenhagen.

Internet Cafes and Coworking Spaces for Digital Nomads: For visitors looking for a quiet and productive environment to access the internet, Copenhagen is home to numerous internet cafes and coworking spaces. These spaces provide high-speed internet access, comfortable working environments, and additional services like printing, scanning, and private meeting rooms. Many of these coworking spaces are located in the city's vibrant districts, including Nørrebro, Vesterbro, and Frederiksberg, where digital nomads and business travelers alike can find a welcoming atmosphere to work, collaborate, or simply get some work done while traveling. Some popular coworking spaces, such as Founders House and Republikken, offer daily passes that allow you to use their facilities without committing to long-term memberships. These spaces not only provide reliable internet connectivity but also foster a sense of community, where travelers can meet like-minded individuals. In addition to coworking spaces, a number of cafes around Copenhagen also cater to remote workers, offering strong Wi-Fi connections, power outlets, and cozy workstations. This makes Copenhagen an ideal destination for those who want to combine travel with work, whether for a few hours or several days.

Mobile Data Plans for Long-Term Visitors: For those staying in Copenhagen for an extended period or planning to use their phones extensively, purchasing a Danish mobile plan can offer a cost-effective and seamless solution. Providers such as TDC, Telia, and 3 offer affordable monthly data plans that include unlimited calls, text, and generous data allowances. These plans are particularly useful for long-term visitors who want to avoid the hassle of frequently recharging prepaid SIM cards. Mobile data plans can be activated at any mobile store or online, and the process is quick and easy. These plans often come with a wide range of options depending on how much data you need, from basic plans for occasional browsing to more extensive packages for streaming and downloading. Mobile plans can also be paired with home internet services for visitors who require internet connectivity in their accommodations for remote work or entertainment.

5.13 Visitor Centers and Tourist Assistance

To ensure that every traveler has access to the information and support they need, the city boasts a variety of well-equipped visitor centers scattered throughout its most iconic areas. These centers not only provide maps, brochures, and expert advice, but they also offer unique services designed to enhance your travel experience. Whether you are seeking personalized recommendations, booking tours, or simply getting assistance with directions, Copenhagen's visitor centers and tourist assistance services are invaluable for anyone looking to explore the Danish capital with ease and confidence.

The Official Copenhagen Visitor Center at City Hall Square: Located at the heart of Copenhagen, the Copenhagen Visitor Center at Rådhuspladsen, or City Hall Square, is one of the most prominent and easily accessible tourist information points in the city. This visitor center is housed in a beautiful building that blends modern amenities with historical charm. Situated just steps away from the City Hall, a landmark that many tourists pass as they make their way through the city center, the center provides an extensive array of services to help make your visit more enjoyable. Upon entering the Copenhagen Visitor Center, visitors will find an array of brochures and maps, including specific details on walking tours, bike routes, and public transport. The staff, fluent in English and several other languages, are always ready to offer expert advice, give suggestions on local attractions, and help with booking tours and activities. The center also offers Copenhagen City Cards, which provide free access to over 80 attractions, including museums, boat tours, and discounts at restaurants. For visitors looking to make their stay more comfortable, the center also offers details on accommodation options, from budget hostels to luxurious hotels, and can assist with last-minute reservations. The center is open daily, from 9:00 AM to 6:00 PM. It is conveniently located near the Copenhagen Central Station, making it easily accessible for those arriving by train. Whether you're a first-time visitor or a returning traveler, the Copenhagen Visitor Center at Rådhuspladsen is a must-visit stop for anyone looking to get the most out of their time in the city.

The Copenhagen Info Centre at Nyhavn: For those visiting the picturesque district of Nyhavn, a visit to the Copenhagen Info Centre at Nyhavn 1F is highly recommended. Nyhavn is one of the city's most iconic spots, known for its colorful buildings, historic canals, and vibrant atmosphere. The Info Centre here caters to visitors who want information on both the city and its waterways. It is particularly helpful for tourists looking to explore the harbor via boat tours, or those interested in learning about the city's maritime history. The center offers brochures on various boat trips, including canal tours and harbor cruises, and has detailed information on surrounding attractions such as The Little Mermaid, Amalienborg Palace, and Tivoli Gardens. The knowledgeable staff provides assistance in booking tours, purchasing tickets, and finding accommodations, making it easier to explore the area and its offerings without wasting time. The center also provides a selection of souvenirs, including postcards and unique Danish-designed gifts, allowing visitors to take a piece of Copenhagen home with them. The Copenhagen Info Centre at Nyhavn operates from 9:00 AM to 6:00 PM, with extended hours during the tourist season. It is easily reachable by walking from Kongens Nytorv, which is also well connected by metro, bus, and ferry.

The Copenhagen Tourist Information Center at Copenhagen Central Station: The Copenhagen Tourist Information Center is situated within the Copenhagen Central Station, one of the busiest transport hubs in Denmark. This central location makes it an ideal stop for visitors arriving by train or those who want to get oriented with the city's public transportation options. It is located on the ground floor of the station, near the main entrance, and serves as a one-stop-shop for visitors in need of assistance as they begin their exploration of Copenhagen. At this center, visitors can pick up free brochures, maps, and timetables for public transport, including details about the metro, buses, and regional trains. Staff members are ready to answer questions about transportation routes, recommend sightseeing spots, and provide up-to-date information on city events, exhibitions, and festivals. The center also offers a ticket service for public transport, where tourists can buy City Pass cards that allow for unlimited travel within certain zones, as well as the Copenhagen Card for access to multiple attractions. For visitors interested in booking tours, the center also offers information about hop-on-hop-off buses, guided bike tours, and walking tours that cover the city's most famous landmarks. Open daily from 9:00 AM to 5:00 PM, the Copenhagen Tourist Information Center is perfect for travelers arriving at the central station or those looking for easy access to public transit information.

Frederiksberg's Tourist Information at Frederiksberg Garden: A slightly off-the-beaten-path gem, the Frederiksberg Tourist Information located near Frederiksberg Garden offers a more local experience for those looking to explore the residential and cultural side of Copenhagen. Situated at Frederiksberg Runddel, just a short walk from the stunning park, this center is ideal for visitors who wish to experience the quieter, charming districts outside of the central tourist areas. It's a great starting point for exploring the beautiful Frederiksberg Gardens, the impressive Frederiksberg Palace, and the nearby Copenhagen Zoo. In addition to offering maps and brochures, the staff at the Frederiksberg Tourist Information Center are experts on the local area and can provide personalized recommendations for lesser-known gems, such as hidden cafes, local art galleries, and charming shops. They also offer advice on public transportation routes that connect Frederiksberg to the city center and other popular tourist destinations. Visitors can easily reach this center by metro, bus, or a short bicycle ride from the city center, making it an accessible stop for those wanting a different perspective of Copenhagen. The Frederiksberg Tourist Information operates from 10:00 AM to 5:00 PM, and the staff here go out of their way to ensure visitors have a unique and enriching experience of Copenhagen's lesser-explored districts.

CHAPTER 6
GASTRONOMIC DELIGHTS

6.1 Dining Options and Top Restaurants

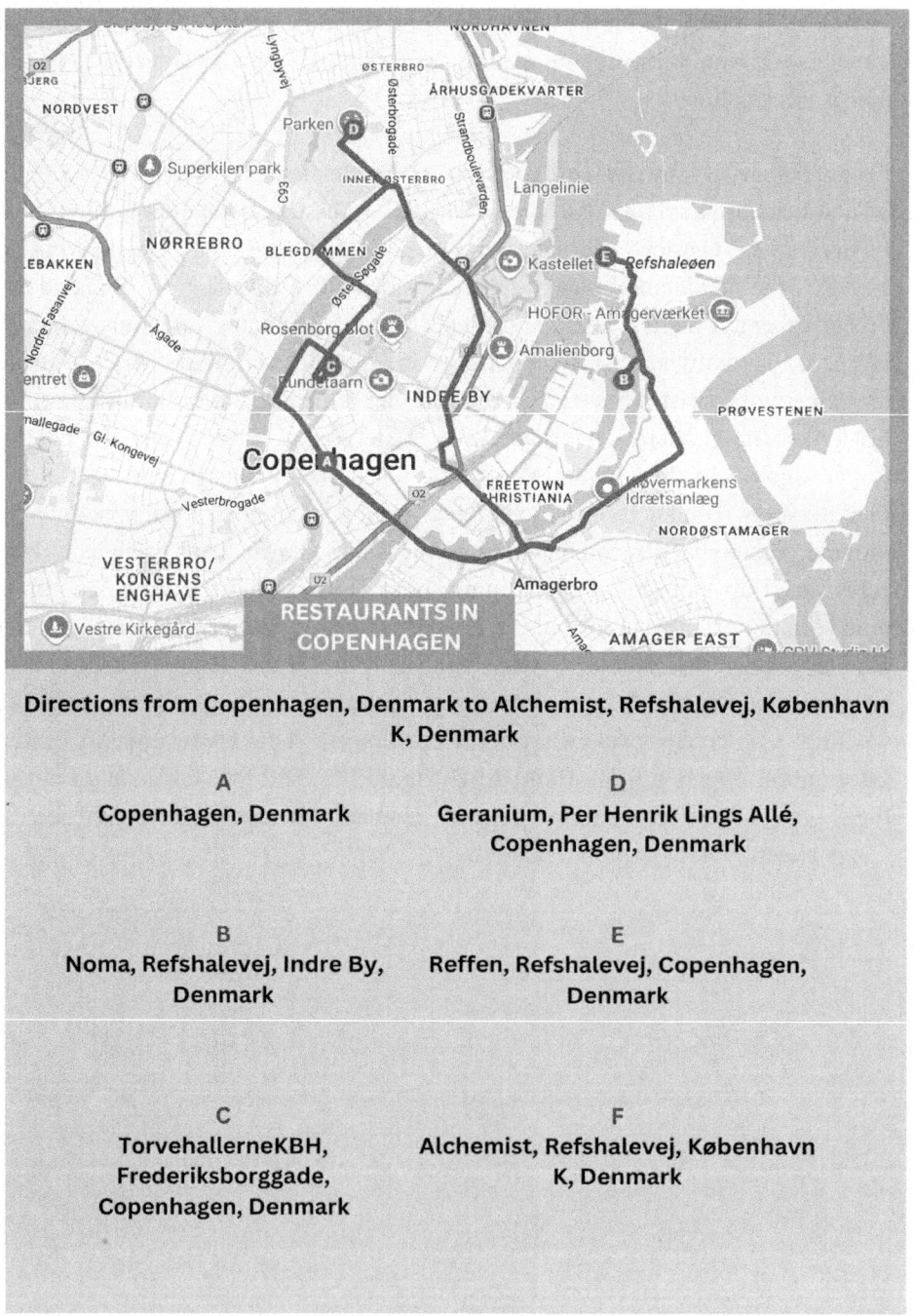

Directions from Copenhagen, Denmark to Alchemist, Refshalevej, København K, Denmark

A
Copenhagen, Denmark

D
Geranium, Per Henrik Lings Allé, Copenhagen, Denmark

B
Noma, Refshalevej, Indre By, Denmark

E
Reffen, Refshalevej, Copenhagen, Denmark

C
TorvehallerneKBH, Frederiksborggade, Copenhagen, Denmark

F
Alchemist, Refshalevej, København K, Denmark

Copenhagen, a city celebrated for its world-class dining scene, is a paradise for food enthusiasts. From Michelin-starred restaurants to cozy neighborhood eateries, the Danish capital offers an array of culinary delights that cater to diverse tastes and budgets. In this detailed guide, we explore five exceptional dining options, each offering a unique gastronomic experience.

Noma: Along Refshalevej, Noma has firmly established itself as a global icon of Nordic gastronomy. Helmed by Chef René Redzepi, this three-Michelin-star restaurant showcases a menu that evolves with the seasons. Diners are treated to an innovative array of dishes, highlighting ingredients sourced from Denmark's forests, fields, and waters. Expect exquisite offerings like fermented mushrooms, freshly foraged herbs, and seafood prepared with unparalleled precision. Noma operates on a pre-booked, multi-course dining model, with prices starting at around 3,200 DKK per person, excluding wine pairings. The restaurant is known for its intimate, minimalist decor that mirrors the Nordic aesthetic, creating an immersive dining experience. Noma opens from 12:00 PM to 4:00 PM for lunch and 6:00 PM to 11:00 PM for dinner, Tuesday through Saturday. Reservations are essential and are often booked months in advance.

Torvehallerne: For those seeking a more casual yet equally delightful culinary adventure, Torvehallerne food market on Frederiksborggade is a must-visit. This bustling market comprises over 60 stalls offering everything from fresh seafood to organic produce and artisanal Danish pastries. Smørrebrød, the traditional open-faced sandwich, is a highlight here, with a variety of toppings like pickled herring, roast beef, and creamy potato salad. Visitors can also enjoy a wide range of beverages, including freshly brewed coffee, local craft beer, and organic juices. Prices vary but remain relatively affordable, with most dishes costing between 50 and 150 DKK. Torvehallerne is open from 10:00 AM to 7:00 PM daily, making it an excellent choice for breakfast, lunch, or a quick snack. Its vibrant atmosphere and central location make it a popular spot for locals and tourists alike.

Geranium: Located on the eighth floor of Parken Stadium in Per Henrik Lings Allé, Geranium is the only restaurant in Denmark to hold three Michelin stars. Chef Rasmus Kofoed's creations are a testament to the artistry of fine dining, with a menu that harmoniously combines local ingredients with a modern, minimalist approach. Signature dishes include langoustine with dill and cucumber and a dessert medley featuring Nordic berries. The restaurant offers wine and juice pairings that perfectly complement the intricate flavors of its menu. Dining at Geranium is a luxurious experience, with a tasting menu priced at approximately 3,600 DKK. Geranium is open for lunch from 12:00 PM to 4:00 PM and for dinner from 6:00 PM to 11:00 PM, Wednesday through Saturday. Reservations are highly recommended to secure a table at this culinary masterpiece.

Reffen: Reffen, located in Refshaleøen, is Copenhagen's largest street food market, offering a vibrant and eclectic dining experience. This open-air market is home to over 50 food stalls and trucks serving global cuisines, including Thai curries, Italian wood-fired pizzas, and Middle Eastern falafels. Vegan and vegetarian options abound, ensuring everyone finds something to enjoy. Drinks range from craft cocktails and local beers to refreshing lemonades, all served with a view of the harbor. Prices at Reffen are wallet-friendly, with most meals priced between 75 and 150 DKK. The market is open from 11:00 AM to 10:00 PM during the warmer months, from April to October. Its laid-back vibe and scenic waterfront location make it a favorite spot for a casual meal or an evening hangout.

Alchemist: For an extraordinary dining experience that transcends traditional boundaries, Alchemist on Refshalevej offers a theatrical and multisensory journey. Chef Rasmus Munk's two-Michelin-starred establishment presents a 50-course menu that blends art, science, and cuisine. Diners might encounter edible illusions, interactive presentations, and flavors that challenge preconceived notions of food. Alchemist's extensive wine list and creative non-alcoholic pairings complement its avant-garde dishes. Prices for this unparalleled experience start at 4,000 DKK per person, with additional charges for beverage pairings. The restaurant operates from 5:00 PM to 11:00 PM, Wednesday through Saturday, and reservations are mandatory. Its unique approach to dining ensures a once-in-a-lifetime experience that leaves an indelible impression.

6.2 Danish Cuisine and Local Specialties (Smørrebrød, Flæskesteg)

Copenhagen is a treasure trove of culinary delights. The city's food culture embodies the charm of traditional Danish flavors, harmonized with modern innovation. For visitors, indulging in local specialties is more than just a meal—it's an immersion into the history, culture, and essence of Danish life. Iconic dishes like smørrebrød and flæskesteg are more than just staples; they are cultural ambassadors, carrying stories of the land and sea that define Denmark's heritage. In Copenhagen, these beloved dishes are celebrated with creativity and authenticity in venues ranging from cozy eateries to upscale restaurants.

Smørrebrød: At the heart of Danish cuisine lies smørrebrød, an open-faced sandwich that turns simplicity into artistry. Traditionally built on slices of dense rye bread, smørrebrød is topped with an array of carefully arranged ingredients such as pickled herring, cured meats, fresh herbs, and vibrant vegetables. These sandwiches are not just a meal but a feast for the eyes, served with meticulous attention to detail. One of the best places to enjoy smørrebrød in Copenhagen is Restaurant Schønnemann, a historic establishment located near Kongens Nytorv. With roots dating back to 1877, this restaurant is revered for its authentic take on Danish classics. The menu offers a variety of options, including marinated herring with capers and egg yolk, or roast beef with pickles and remoulade. Prices for smørrebrød range from DKK 85 to DKK 150 per piece, with each sandwich large enough to serve as a meal.

Flæskesteg: No exploration of Danish cuisine is complete without tasting flæskesteg, a succulent roasted pork dish traditionally served with crispy crackling, caramelized potatoes, and red cabbage. Flæskesteg is not just a meal—it's a cornerstone of Danish celebrations, from Christmas feasts to family gatherings. For an unforgettable flæskesteg experience, head to Restaurant Puk, a charming venue tucked away near the City Hall Square. This restaurant serves a hearty rendition of flæskesteg with all the trimmings, offering diners a taste of homestyle Danish cooking. A plate of flæskesteg here costs around DKK 195, making it a fulfilling yet affordable way to enjoy this iconic dish. Visitors should note that flæskesteg is often featured on daily specials or as part of a traditional Danish dinner menu. To elevate the experience, try pairing the dish with a glass of house-made schnapps. The warm, rustic ambiance of Restaurant Puk adds to the charm, making it a must-visit for anyone seeking an authentic taste of Denmark.

Frikadeller: Another beloved staple of Danish cuisine is frikadeller, savory meatballs made from a mixture of pork and veal, flavored with onions, breadcrumbs, and spices. Served with potatoes, gravy, and a side of pickled cucumbers, frikadeller embodies the comforting flavors of Danish home cooking. For a hearty serving of frikadeller, visit Grøften, an iconic eatery located within Tivoli Gardens. Established in 1874, Grøften is a haven of traditional Danish fare and is especially famous for its generous portions and warm hospitality. A plate of frikadeller here costs approximately DKK 160 and is large enough to satisfy even the hungriest traveler. Tivoli Gardens' magical ambiance makes dining at Grøften a unique experience. Visitors are encouraged to explore the gardens before or after their meal, adding an enchanting backdrop to their culinary adventure.

Rugbrød: Rugbrød, Denmark's beloved rye bread, is more than just an accompaniment—it's the cornerstone of Danish cuisine. Dense, flavorful, and packed with nutrients, rugbrød serves as the base for many dishes, including smørrebrød. Its rich, earthy flavor pairs perfectly with the tanginess of pickled toppings or the creaminess of butter. For a taste of freshly baked rugbrød, stop by Hart Bageri, a modern bakery in Frederiksberg that has gained a reputation for elevating traditional Danish breadmaking. Here, rugbrød is baked to perfection, using a blend of organic rye flour and sourdough starter. A loaf costs around DKK 50 and makes for an excellent souvenir or picnic essential.

Æbleskiver: While exploring Danish cuisine, don't miss æbleskiver, a traditional Danish dessert that resembles round, fluffy pancakes. Typically served during the holiday season, these delightful treats are made with a batter infused with vanilla and cardamom, cooked in a special pan to achieve their characteristic spherical shape. They are served hot, dusted with powdered sugar, and accompanied by jam. The best place to try æbleskiver in Copenhagen is La Glace, a historic patisserie in the city center. Known for its desserts, La Glace offers a seasonal menu featuring æbleskiver during winter, priced at around DKK 75 for a portion of three. Visitors can enjoy these alongside a cup of Danish hot chocolate or gløgg (mulled wine) for the ultimate indulgence.

6.3 Street Food and Markets

These vibrant hubs of flavor offer a delicious journey into Danish and international cuisines, catering to foodies and curious travelers alike. Exploring these spaces provides a chance to savor diverse dishes, interact with locals, and immerse yourself in Copenhagen's culinary culture. Below are essential street food and market experiences, each with its unique charm and culinary treasures.

Reffen: Located on Refshaleøen, Reffen is a sprawling street food market that embodies Copenhagen's innovative spirit. Set in a former industrial area overlooking the harbor, Reffen combines culinary diversity with sustainability. The market features over 50 stalls offering food from around the world. Whether you're craving spicy Mexican tacos, authentic Italian pizza, fragrant Thai curries, or local Danish smørrebrød, Reffen has something to tantalize every taste bud. Prices here are relatively affordable, with most dishes costing between 75 to 150 DKK, making it ideal for those exploring on a budget. Reffen also boasts an impressive selection of craft beers, organic wines, and creative cocktails to complement your meal. The market operates seasonally, typically opening from April to October, from 11 AM to 10 PM on weekdays and until midnight on weekends. Its unique industrial-meets-nature vibe and waterfront views make it a favorite among locals and tourists alike.

Torvehallerne: Situated in the heart of Copenhagen near Nørreport Station, Torvehallerne is a high-end food market that caters to those seeking quality and authenticity. With over 60 stalls housed in two sleek glass pavilions, this market is a feast for the senses. From freshly baked Danish pastries to artisanal cheeses, organic produce, and locally sourced seafood, Torvehallerne offers an extensive range of gourmet delights. One of the must-try spots is Hallernes Smørrebrød, where you can savor traditional open-faced sandwiches topped with herring, roast beef, or seasonal vegetables. For dessert, Summerbird's luxurious chocolates and flødeboller are a treat. While prices are slightly higher here, ranging from 100 to 200 DKK per dish, the quality of ingredients and preparation justifies the cost. Torvehallerne is open daily from 10 AM to 7 PM, though the energy peaks around lunchtime when locals flock in for a quick yet satisfying bite.

Broens Gadekøkken: Located near the picturesque Nyhavn, Broens Gadekøkken, or Bridge Street Kitchen, is an intimate yet lively food market that perfectly blends Copenhagen's urban and maritime vibes. The market is compact but features a curated selection of food trucks and stalls serving global and Nordic flavors. You can indulge in gourmet burgers, Korean fried chicken, Indian curries, and even vegan specialties. Drink options include local beers, fresh juices, and natural wines, making it a great place to unwind. Dishes here typically cost between 75 to 125 DKK, and the market prides itself on using organic and sustainable ingredients. Open from April to September, Broens Gadekøkken operates from 11:30 AM to 9 PM daily, with extended hours during summer weekends. The setting, overlooking the water and close to the famous bridge linking Nyhavn and Christianshavn, makes this market a memorable culinary stop.

WestMarket: Located in Vesterbro, WestMarket is an indoor market that exudes a more local and laid-back atmosphere. This market is a melting pot of cultures, reflecting the neighborhood's diversity. It offers a mix of traditional Danish snacks, such as hot dogs and Danish pastries, alongside international cuisines, including Middle Eastern falafel, Japanese sushi, and Italian gelato. WestMarket is also a great spot for breakfast, with coffee and fresh pastries served at several stalls. Prices range from 50 to 150 DKK, making it an affordable option for sampling a variety of dishes. The market opens daily from 10 AM to 8 PM, with some stalls and eateries extending their hours into the evening. Beyond food, WestMarket hosts occasional events, including live music and pop-up shops, adding to its dynamic vibe.

Paper Island (Papirøen): Although the original Paper Island closed, its legacy lives on in a newly revived form on Refshaleøen, where it continues to attract food enthusiasts. This reincarnation features a vibrant collection of food stalls offering everything from Danish meatballs to Caribbean jerk chicken and

Japanese ramen. It is a true paradise for those seeking bold and diverse flavors. The atmosphere is electric, with communal seating areas that encourage socializing and a backdrop of creative street art and performances. Prices for dishes range from 75 to 150 DKK. The market is open from 11 AM to 10 PM daily, extending later on weekends. What sets this venue apart is its commitment to sustainability, with many vendors focusing on eco-friendly practices.

6.4 Coffee Culture and Cafes

Copenhagen boasts a coffee culture as rich and textured as its history. Known for its hygge-filled cafés and artisanal coffee, the city offers visitors an array of cozy spots that go beyond caffeine to create experiences. From minimalist interiors to decadent pastries, these cafés reflect Copenhagen's blend of tradition and innovation. Here, we explore must-visit coffee havens in the city, each with its own charm, culinary delights, and unique ambiance.

The Coffee Collective (Godthåbsvej): The Coffee Collective, in the Frederiksberg district, is a pioneer of Copenhagen's coffee culture. Renowned for its sustainable practices, this café sources beans directly from farmers, ensuring ethical and flavorful brews. Upon entering, visitors are greeted by a minimalist yet warm design, with a focus on open spaces and natural light. The menu here is a haven for coffee purists. From expertly brewed espressos to velvety lattes, every cup showcases the baristas' precision. Their signature hand-poured filter coffee offers a chance to savor the nuanced flavors of single-origin beans. Pair your drink with a flaky croissant or a Danish tebirkes—a local pastry filled with marzipan. Prices range from 35 DKK for an espresso to 65 DKK for more elaborate beverages. Unique to the Coffee Collective is their on-site roasting facility, which allows customers to witness the journey of the bean from roast to cup. Open daily from 7:30 AM to 6:00 PM, this café is a beacon for anyone seeking a deeper connection to their coffee.

The Paludan Bog & Café: Located near the University of Copenhagen, Paludan Bog & Café merges literature and coffee in a quintessentially Danish way. This bookshop café invites patrons to lose themselves among shelves of books while sipping aromatic brews. It's a place where academics, students, and travelers mingle, creating a vibrant yet intimate atmosphere. Paludan's menu is diverse, offering something for everyone. Coffee options include cappuccinos, cortados, and chai lattes, all priced between 40 and 60 DKK. The food offerings extend beyond pastries to include hearty sandwiches, salads, and a highly recommended Danish smørrebrød. Their carrot cake, at 55 DKK per slice, is a crowd favorite. Open from 9:00 AM to 10:00 PM, Paludan is more than a café—it's a cultural institution. With free Wi-Fi and a setting perfect for writing or people-watching, it's a sanctuary for those seeking inspiration.

Andersen & Maillard: In the hipster haven of Nørrebro, Andersen & Maillard elevates coffee culture with its fusion of craft baking and specialty coffee. The industrial-chic space, with exposed concrete and wooden accents, sets the stage for culinary artistry. The café's signature is its combination of expertly brewed coffee and house-made pastries. Their espresso tonic is a refreshing twist, while the classic flat white is a creamy delight. Prices range from 40 DKK for a basic coffee to 75 DKK for specialty drinks. The pastries, particularly the croissants and cardamom buns, are baked fresh daily, with prices starting at 35 DKK. Open from 7:30 AM to 5:00 PM, Andersen & Maillard is an Instagram-worthy destination. Its outdoor seating area is ideal for sunny mornings, while its cozy indoor ambiance offers refuge on cooler days.

Democratic Coffee: Tucked inside the Copenhagen Main Library, Democratic Coffee is a testament to the city's emphasis on quality and simplicity. This café is a favorite among locals who cherish its unpretentious vibe and consistently excellent coffee. Specializing in single-origin beans, Democratic Coffee offers a range of hand-brewed coffees and espresso-based drinks. Their filter coffee, priced at 40 DKK, is particularly notable for its clarity of flavor. The café's almond croissants, freshly baked each morning, are legendary among Copenhagenites. Open from 9:00 AM to 6:00 PM on weekdays and 10:00 AM to 4:00 PM on Saturdays, this spot is perfect for anyone seeking a quiet, contemplative coffee experience. With views of book-lined walls and natural light streaming in, Democratic Coffee invites visitors to slow down and savor the moment.

Prolog Coffee Bar: Prolog Coffee Bar, located in the trendy Meatpacking District, is a boutique café known for its meticulous approach to coffee. The small yet welcoming space is adorned with modern Scandinavian décor, creating a warm and inviting atmosphere. Prolog's menu reflects its focus on precision. From silky flat whites to refreshing cold brews, each cup is crafted with care. Prices hover between 40 and 60 DKK. The café also offers a selection of gourmet chocolates and light snacks, such as granola bars and Danish cookies, making it an ideal pit stop for a quick indulgence. Open daily from 8:00 AM to

5:00 PM, Prolog Coffee Bar is beloved for its knowledgeable baristas who are eager to share insights about brewing methods and flavor profiles. It's a must-visit for true coffee aficionados exploring Copenhagen.

6.5 Cooking Classes and Culinary Workshops

These experiences provide a hands-on approach to Danish cuisine, as well as insights into international flavors, all while uncovering the secrets behind the city's culinary reputation. From traditional Nordic dishes to fusion creations, these workshops cater to every food enthusiast's curiosity and palate.

Copenhagen Cooking School: In the heart of the city, Copenhagen Cooking School is an oasis for food lovers eager to explore the intricacies of Danish cuisine. Located in Frederiksberg, this culinary institution specializes in showcasing the flavors of New Nordic cooking—a movement rooted in local, seasonal, and sustainable ingredients. Participants learn to prepare traditional dishes such as smørrebrød (open-faced sandwiches) and foraged herb salads, alongside modern interpretations like smoked fish with horseradish cream and beetroot reductions. The school offers both single-day classes and intensive weekend workshops. Prices range from DKK 900 to DKK 1,500, depending on the program. Classes generally run from 10:00 AM to 3:00 PM, ensuring ample time to master techniques and savor creations over a shared meal. What sets Copenhagen Cooking School apart is its emphasis on storytelling—chefs delve into the history and cultural significance of each recipe, making the experience as enriching as it is flavorful.

Timm Vladimir's Kitchen: For those seeking a relaxed and social culinary adventure, Timm Vladimir's Kitchen in Valby offers an eclectic mix of classes that highlight both Danish staples and global cuisine. Run by Danish TV personality Timm Vladimir, this venue prides itself on being a hub for creativity and camaraderie. The workshops here include a wide range of themes, from sushi rolling to mastering Italian pasta, alongside traditional Danish baking sessions.Wine pairing is a highlight, with sommelier-guided tastings complementing many workshops. Prices range from DKK 1,000 to DKK 1,800, and classes typically run in the evenings from 5:30 PM to 9:00 PM, making it a perfect after-work or vacation evening activity. Guests often praise the lively atmosphere and Timm's charismatic teaching style, which creates a sense of community among participants.

Culinary Experience Copenhagen: For food enthusiasts with a passion for sustainability, Culinary Experience Copenhagen, located in Østerbro, is an ideal choice. This workshop focuses on teaching participants how to craft delicious, eco-friendly dishes using locally sourced and organic ingredients. The menus feature plant-based delicacies like pickled root vegetables, mushroom pâté, and hearty grain bowls, alongside sustainable seafood options such as cured trout and seaweed salads. Workshops are held in a beautifully designed studio kitchen with a focus on hands-on learning. Prices vary from DKK 800 for a two-hour class to DKK 2,000 for an all-day session that includes visits to local markets and farms. The classes operate mainly during the weekends, from 11:00 AM to 4:00 PM, giving attendees plenty of time to immerse themselves in Copenhagen's green culinary culture. The unique feature of this workshop is its "zero waste" philosophy, where participants learn creative ways to utilize every part of an ingredient.

Copenhagen Food Tours: Copenhagen Food Tours elevates the typical culinary class by integrating local sightseeing with cooking experiences. Their "Hotel-Home Cooking" workshops take place in cozy kitchens set up within historic locations across the city, including Nyhavn and Vesterbro. These workshops provide visitors with an intimate experience of Danish hospitality as they learn to cook authentic dishes like frikadeller (meatballs) and æbleskiver (Danish pancakes). Each session includes a tasting of regional beers and aquavit, enhancing the cultural immersion. Prices are set at DKK 1,200 per person, with sessions lasting three hours and available from 2:00 PM to 5:00 PM. The standout feature of this experience is the personal connection participants forge with their hosts, who often share their own family recipes and stories.

The Bread Basket Copenhagen: Bread lovers flock to The Bread Basket Copenhagen, a bakery and culinary workshop located in Nørrebro. This intimate space specializes in teaching the art of Danish bread-making, from sourdough techniques to crafting rye bread (rugbrød) and delicate pastries like kanelsnegle (cinnamon rolls). Guests can also explore gluten-free options and innovative recipes incorporating Nordic grains.The workshops are offered at various levels, from beginner to advanced, ensuring everyone can enjoy the process of kneading and baking. Prices range from DKK 700 for a two-hour class to DKK 1,200 for an extended session that includes multiple recipes and a full baking toolkit to take home.

6.6 Nightlife and Entertainment

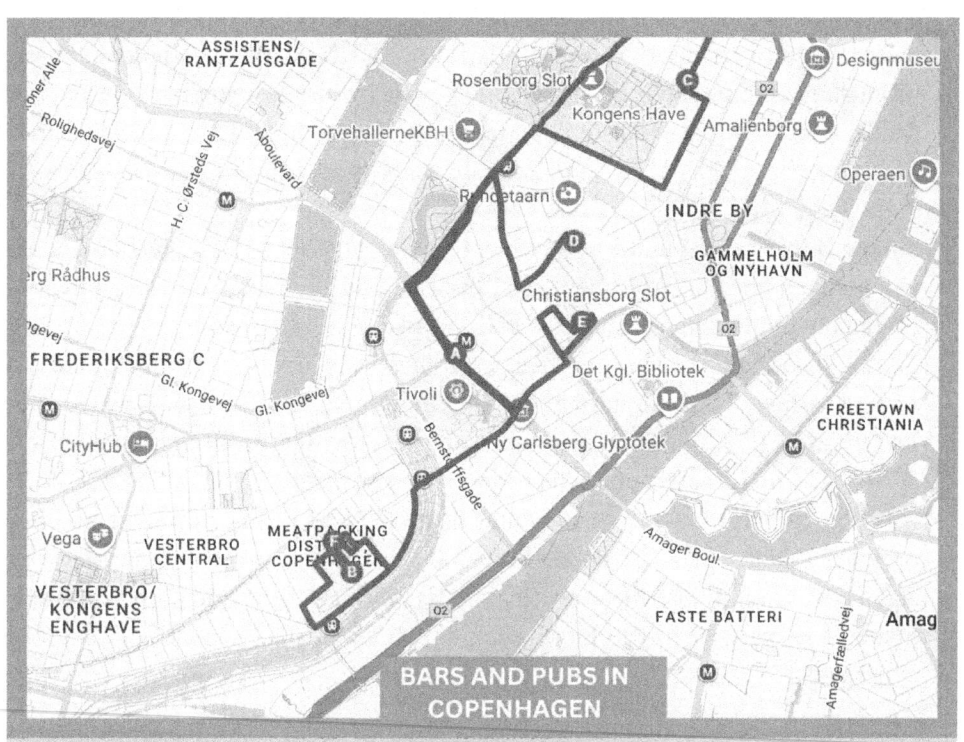

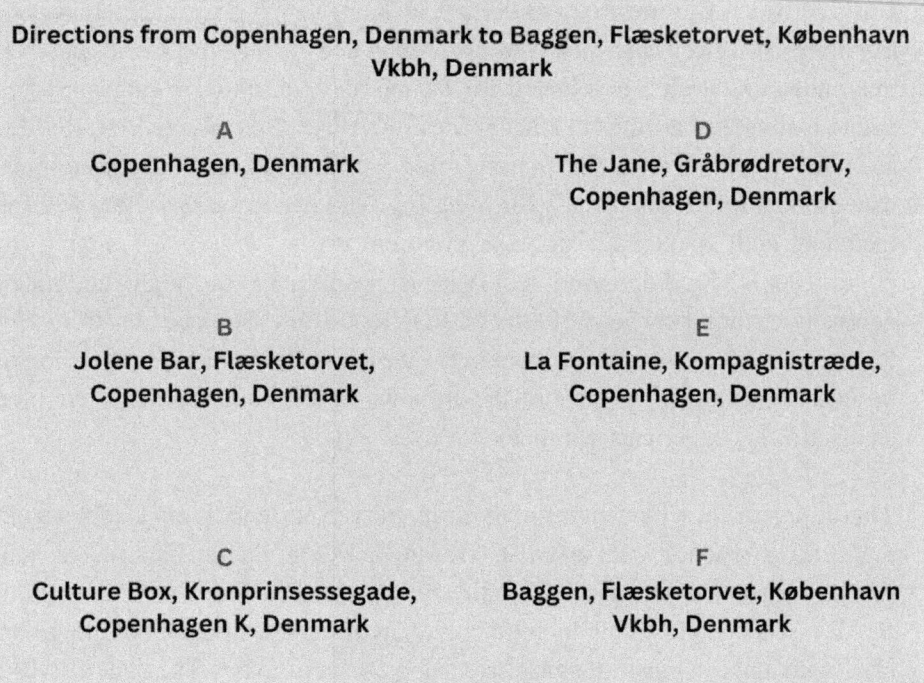

BARS AND PUBS IN COPENHAGEN

Directions from Copenhagen, Denmark to Baggen, Flæsketorvet, København Vkbh, Denmark

A
Copenhagen, Denmark

B
Jolene Bar, Flæsketorvet, Copenhagen, Denmark

C
Culture Box, Kronprinsessegade, Copenhagen K, Denmark

D
The Jane, Gråbrødretorv, Copenhagen, Denmark

E
La Fontaine, Kompagnistræde, Copenhagen, Denmark

F
Baggen, Flæsketorvet, København Vkbh, Denmark

Copenhagen, with its dynamic cultural landscape and vibrant urban vibe, offers a rich nightlife scene that caters to all tastes. From electrifying clubs to cozy jazz bars, the city comes alive after dark. Each venue has its unique charm, promising unforgettable evenings filled with music, dancing, and exceptional drinks. Here's an in-depth look at five remarkable nightlife and entertainment spots that capture the essence of Copenhagen's after-hours allure.

Jolene Bar: Located in the trendy Meatpacking District of Vesterbro, Jolene Bar is a beloved hotspot for Copenhagen's artistic and alternative crowd. Known for its unpretentious atmosphere and eclectic playlist, Jolene offers a mix of funk, disco, house, and indie beats spun by local and international DJs. The bar features a raw, industrial aesthetic with dim lighting, graffiti-strewn walls, and a lively dance floor. Drinks are affordably priced, with creative cocktails starting at 80 DKK and a selection of beers and wines available for 50 to 70 DKK. Food isn't served here, but the surrounding district offers plenty of pre-party dining options. Jolene opens its doors from 5:00 PM to 2:00 AM on weekdays and stays open until 4:00 AM on weekends. Its laid-back vibe and pulsating energy make it a must-visit for those seeking an authentic Copenhagen nightlife experience.

Culture Box: Culture Box, situated near Kongens Nytorv, is the epicenter of Copenhagen's electronic music scene. Renowned for hosting world-class DJs, this underground club is a haven for techno and house music enthusiasts. The venue is divided into four distinct spaces: the Black Box, White Box, Red Box, and a cozy lounge area. Each space offers a unique atmosphere, from intense dance floors to quieter corners for mingling. The bar serves a variety of drinks, including craft cocktails, beers, and premium spirits, with prices ranging from 60 to 100 DKK. Admission fees vary depending on the night and lineup, generally costing between 150 and 250 DKK. Culture Box operates from 10:00 PM to 6:00 AM on weekends, making it the go-to destination for those looking to dance until dawn. Its state-of-the-art sound system and top-tier talent create an electrifying experience for music lovers.

The Jane: In the city center on Gråbrødretorv, The Jane offers a sophisticated nightlife experience with a twist. Designed like a classic library, the venue exudes elegance with its leather chairs, vintage bookshelves, and warm lighting. By day, it feels like a chic lounge, but as night falls, it transforms into a lively club with upbeat music ranging from pop to deep house. The Jane serves an impressive menu of expertly crafted cocktails, starting at 120 DKK, alongside premium wines and champagne. For a more indulgent experience, guests can opt for bottle service in the VIP area. The venue opens from 5:00 PM to midnight on weekdays and stays open until 3:00 AM on weekends. Its seamless blend of sophistication and energy makes it a favorite among Copenhagen's stylish crowd.

La Fontaine: La Fontaine, located in the heart of the city on Skindergade, is Copenhagen's oldest jazz club and a cherished spot for live music lovers. With its intimate setting, dimly lit interior, and exceptional acoustics, La Fontaine provides an enchanting atmosphere for an evening of smooth tunes. Live performances by talented local and international jazz musicians take place nightly, often accompanied by impromptu jam sessions. The bar offers a selection of beers, wines, and spirits, with prices ranging from 50 to 80 DKK. While the focus is on the music, a small menu of light snacks is available to complement the drinks. Entry fees vary, typically costing around 80 DKK for the night. La Fontaine is open from 8:00 PM to 2:00 AM during the week, extending to 3:00 AM on weekends. Its soulful ambiance and world-class music make it an essential stop for a relaxed yet captivating nightlife experience.

Bakken Kbh: Hidden in the vibrant Meatpacking District, Bakken Kbh is a quirky bar and live music venue that embodies Copenhagen's creative spirit. The venue hosts an array of events, from live bands and open-mic nights to DJ sets and themed parties. Its casual, artsy decor and welcoming vibe attract a diverse crowd looking for good music and a good time. Bakken Kbh features a reasonably priced drink menu, with craft beers at 50 DKK and cocktails starting at 75 DKK. Though food is not served on-site, the venue is surrounded by excellent restaurants for a pre-night-out meal. Open from 4:00 PM to 2:00 AM on weekdays and until 4:00 AM on weekends, Bakken Kbh is a dynamic spot where creativity and nightlife collide. Its ever-changing lineup ensures that every visit offers something new and exciting.

6.7 Craft Beer and Breweries

Copenhagen is not just a hub for culinary innovation and historic charm; it is also a paradise for craft beer lovers. The city's thriving beer scene combines centuries-old brewing traditions with modern creativity, offering a rich tapestry of flavors and experiences. Breweries and beer bars are scattered across the city, each with its distinct atmosphere and signature brews. Below, we dive into five outstanding craft beer spots in Copenhagen that every visitor should explore, detailing their location, offerings, unique characteristics, and all the practical information you need.

Mikkeller Bar: Located on Viktoriagade in the trendy Vesterbro district, Mikkeller Bar is a name synonymous with the craft beer revolution in Copenhagen. Founded by Mikkel Borg Bjergsø, this iconic bar is a gateway to a world of innovative brewing. Mikkeller Bar features an ever-changing menu of 20 taps, showcasing their in-house creations as well as collaborations with breweries worldwide. From rich imperial stouts and tangy sours to crisp lagers and fruity IPAs, the selection is nothing short of extraordinary. Food here is light but satisfying, often focused on beer-pairing snacks like cheese platters, charcuterie, and gourmet hot dogs. Prices for a pint range from 60 to 90 DKK, reflecting the high quality and creativity of the brews. The bar opens daily, from 2 PM to midnight during weekdays and extending until 2 AM on weekends. Its minimalist interior and focus on beer culture make it a must-visit for enthusiasts eager to delve deep into Denmark's craft beer heritage.

Warpigs Brewpub: In the Meatpacking District, Warpigs Brewpub is a unique collaboration between Mikkeller and the American brewery 3 Floyds. This industrial-style brewpub combines Southern-style barbecue with award-winning beers, creating a bold and hearty experience. The brewpub offers an impressive array of beers brewed on-site, including hoppy IPAs, robust porters, and experimental sour ales. Pair your pint with smoked brisket, pulled pork, or juicy ribs, all served with traditional sides like mac and cheese or coleslaw. Prices for food range from 100 to 200 DKK, while a pint of beer averages around 65 DKK. Warpigs is open daily, from noon until 11 PM, making it a great spot for lunch, dinner, or an evening hangout. Its vibrant outdoor seating area is especially inviting during the summer months, offering a lively atmosphere and a glimpse into Copenhagen's cosmopolitan yet unpretentious vibe.

BRUS: Located in the hip Nørrebro neighborhood, BRUS is a modern brewery, bar, and restaurant all under one roof. Housed in a former factory, this expansive venue features sleek industrial design, large communal tables, and an open view of the brewing process. BRUS offers a wide variety of beers, from their signature New England IPAs to crisp pilsners and barrel-aged sours. The on-site restaurant complements the beer with an eclectic menu, featuring dishes like Nordic-inspired small plates, fresh seafood, and gourmet burgers. Prices are moderate, with beer starting at 50 DKK per glass and meals ranging from 125 to 250 DKK. Open daily from noon to midnight, BRUS is a lively space that attracts both locals and visitors. Its innovative beer styles and culinary offerings make it a destination for those looking to explore the intersection of brewing and gastronomy.

Nørrebro Bryghus: In the heart of Nørrebro, Nørrebro Bryghus is a microbrewery that champions local ingredients and sustainable practices. This cozy brewery offers a curated selection of classic styles and seasonal specialties, such as their Rye IPA, Milk Stout, and refreshing Witbier. Each beer reflects a commitment to quality and a nod to Danish brewing traditions. The brewery's restaurant serves a menu inspired by Nordic cuisine, with hearty dishes like slow-cooked pork, pickled vegetables, and rye bread, all designed to pair seamlessly with the beers. Prices are accessible, with main courses around 150 DKK and beers starting at 45 DKK. Nørrebro Bryghus is open from 11 AM to 10 PM on weekdays, extending until 11 PM on weekends. The intimate atmosphere and friendly service make it an excellent spot for a relaxed evening or a casual lunch.

To Øl City: To Øl City is a hidden gem located in the suburb of Svinninge, about an hour's journey from central Copenhagen. This sprawling brewery campus is more than just a production facility; it is a creative space where experimental brewing takes center stage. To Øl City offers a wide range of beers, including hazy IPAs, barrel-aged saisons, and complex stouts. Visitors can book tours to explore the brewing process and taste exclusive small-batch releases. The on-site taproom serves beers alongside food trucks offering casual fare like burgers and wood-fired pizzas. Prices for beer range from 50 to 100 DKK, while food options are around 75 to 150 DKK. Opening hours vary depending on events, but the taproom is typically open from Thursday to Sunday. The journey to To Øl City is well worth it for adventurous beer lovers eager to experience cutting-edge brewing in a unique setting.

CHAPTER 7
DAY TRIPS AND EXCURSIONS

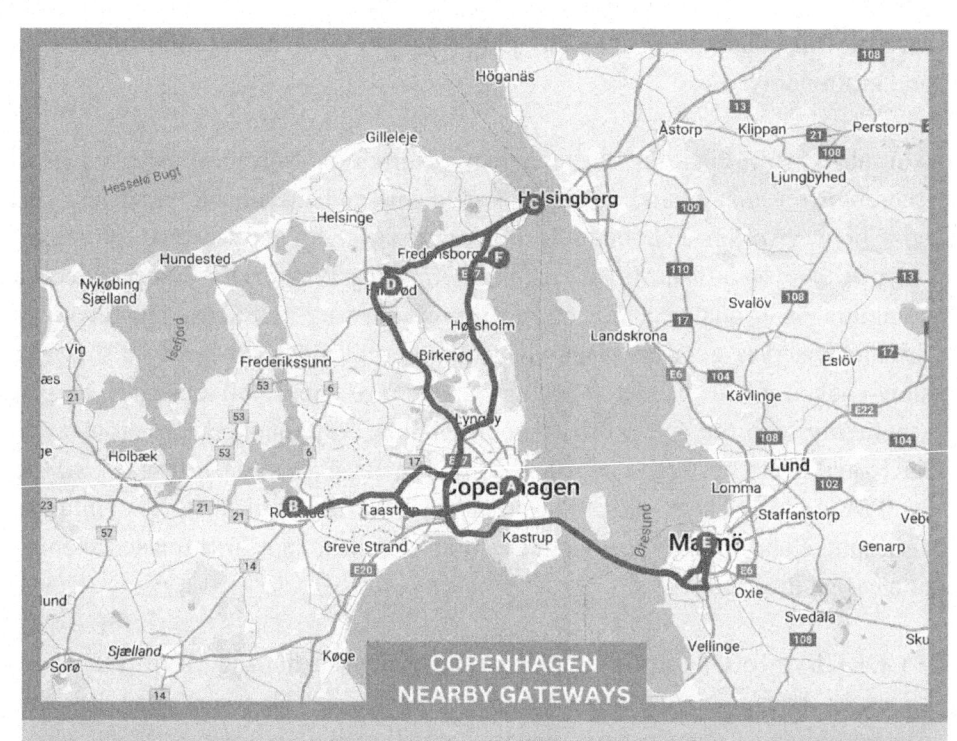

Directions from Copenhagen, Denmark to Louisiana Museum of Modern Art, Gl Strandvej, Humlebaek, Denmark

A
Copenhagen, Denmark

B
Viking Ship Museum, Vindeboder, Roskilde, Denmark

C
Kronborg Castle, Kronborg, Helsingør, Denmark

D
Frederiksborg Castle, Frederiksborg Slot, Hillerød, Denmark

E
Malmö, Sweden

F
Louisiana Museum of Modern Art, Gl Strandvej, Humlebaek, Denmark

7.1 Roskilde and Viking Ship Museum

Roskilde, a charming town just a short distance from Copenhagen, offers a fascinating glimpse into Denmark's medieval past, with its impressive cathedral and renowned Viking Ship Museum. Embarking on a day trip from Copenhagen to this historical town not only allows you to explore these remarkable sites but also provides a beautiful journey through Danish landscapes, enriching your understanding of Viking heritage. Whether you're an avid history enthusiast or simply seeking to immerse yourself in Danish culture, a visit to Roskilde promises an unforgettable experience.

Transportation and Distance: Roskilde is conveniently located approximately 30 kilometers west of Copenhagen, making it an easily accessible destination for day-trippers. The town is well-connected by both train and bus, with a direct train service departing regularly from Copenhagen Central Station. The train ride takes about 25 minutes, offering a comfortable and scenic journey through the Danish countryside. For those seeking a more relaxed and scenic experience, a bus journey is also available, though it takes a little longer, around 35 minutes. For those who prefer driving, renting a car is a viable option. The drive from Copenhagen to Roskilde via the E4 highway is straightforward and takes approximately 40 minutes, providing the flexibility to explore the surroundings at your own pace. Once you arrive, navigating around the town is easy, as Roskilde is small and pedestrian-friendly, making it simple to access the major attractions.

The Viking Ship Museum: No trip to Roskilde would be complete without a visit to the Viking Ship Museum, one of Denmark's most significant historical museums. The museum houses five original Viking ships, each telling a unique story of seafaring adventure, warfare, and trade during the Viking Age. These ships, salvaged from the Roskilde Fjord in the 1960s, are meticulously preserved and displayed, allowing visitors to get up close and personal with Denmark's maritime history. As you enter the Viking Ship Museum, you are greeted by a striking display of the longboats, each one showcasing the craftsmanship and engineering genius of the Vikings. The exhibits delve into the construction methods used by Viking shipbuilders, offering interactive demonstrations that let you appreciate the intricacies of their maritime skills. For those with a keen interest in Viking lore and culture, the museum also provides extensive information on Viking voyages, their encounters with other cultures, and their impact on European history. In addition to the permanent exhibits, the Viking Ship Museum features a range of temporary displays, often highlighting aspects of Viking life such as weapons, clothing, and everyday objects. There is also a chance to engage with live demonstrations and even participate in hands-on activities, like trying your hand at boatbuilding or learning how to row a Viking ship. During the warmer months, the museum offers boat tours where visitors can sail on replica Viking ships, providing an immersive experience of what it was like to journey across the seas during the Viking Age.

The Roskilde Cathedral: While the Viking Ship Museum steals much of the spotlight, Roskilde Cathedral is equally impressive and is well worth a visit. This UNESCO World Heritage Site is one of Denmark's most important religious buildings and a stunning example of Gothic architecture. The cathedral, with its towering spires and intricate stained glass windows, stands as a testament to Denmark's royal history. It has been the burial site of many Danish kings and queens, and as you wander through the cathedral's halls, you can admire the beautifully crafted tombs, each telling a tale of royal lineage and Danish heritage. The cathedral's architecture is a remarkable blend of Romanesque and Gothic styles, featuring soaring arches, detailed sculptures, and elaborate frescoes. Visitors can explore the crypts beneath the cathedral, where members of the Danish royal family are laid to rest, and learn about the historical significance of the church in Denmark's religious and political life. The cathedral is located near the town center, making it easily accessible from the Viking Ship Museum by a short walk through Roskilde's charming streets.

Exploring Roskilde Town: After exploring the Viking Ship Museum and the Roskilde Cathedral, take some time to stroll through the picturesque streets of Roskilde itself. The town has a quaint, small-town feel, with cobblestone streets, colorful buildings, and cozy cafés. You can visit local boutiques, craft shops, and markets, which offer an array of Danish products from locally made jewelry to Viking-inspired souvenirs. The town also boasts several museums and art galleries, adding to its cultural richness. Roskilde is also known for its beautiful parks and green spaces, such as the Roskilde Fjord, where you can enjoy a peaceful walk by the water's edge. The surrounding area offers a relaxing atmosphere, ideal for unwinding after a day filled with historical exploration. If you're visiting in summer, you may be lucky enough to experience some of Roskilde's vibrant festivals, including the famous Roskilde Festival, one of Europe's largest music festivals, which draws thousands of visitors every year.

Practical Information for Visitors: The cost of visiting Roskilde is relatively affordable. A return train ticket from Copenhagen to Roskilde costs approximately DKK 100-150 ($15-20 USD), depending on the type of ticket and discounts available. Entrance to the Viking Ship Museum is around DKK 150-200 ($20-30 USD) for adults, with discounts for children, students, and seniors. Admission to the Roskilde Cathedral is also reasonable, with entry fees typically around DKK 50-60 ($7-8 USD). For those traveling by car, parking in Roskilde is easy to find and reasonably priced, with most attractions offering nearby parking facilities. When planning your visit, be sure to check the opening hours for both the Viking Ship Museum and the Roskilde Cathedral, as these may vary seasonally. The Viking Ship Museum is typically open daily, while the cathedral's hours may depend on religious services and events.

7.2 Kronborg Castle and Helsingør

One of the most remarkable day trips you can take from Copenhagen is to visit the renowned Kronborg Castle in Helsingør, a UNESCO World Heritage site that has captivated visitors for centuries. Located just a short distance from the Danish capital, this excursion offers a rich tapestry of history, culture, and stunning landscapes, making it an unforgettable experience for any traveler.

Distance and Travel Options: The distance from Copenhagen to Helsingør, where Kronborg Castle is located, is approximately 45 kilometers (28 miles). This manageable journey takes around 45 minutes to an hour by car, making it perfect for a day trip. Alternatively, if you prefer to travel by public transport, the regional train service from Copenhagen Central Station to Helsingør takes about 40 minutes, with trains departing regularly throughout the day. For a more scenic route, taking the ferry from Copenhagen to Helsingør provides a relaxing 60-minute journey across the Øresund Strait. The ferry ride not only offers stunning views of the sea but also brings visitors closer to the charming waterfront of Helsingør. For those opting to drive, there is plenty of parking near the castle, while public transportation is equally convenient, with a short walk from Helsingør's train station to the castle itself. The cost of the train ticket is typically around DKK 100 (approximately 15 USD) for a round-trip, while the ferry may cost a little more, depending on the time and class of travel chosen. These transportation options ensure that the journey to Helsingør is both affordable and accessible, catering to all kinds of travelers.

Kronborg Castle: Kronborg Castle, often referred to as Hamlet's Castle due to its connection to Shakespeare's famous play, stands as a formidable sentinel on the shores of the Øresund Strait. Originally built in the 16th century by King Frederick II, the castle played a pivotal role in controlling the trade routes between the Baltic Sea and the North Sea. It was here that Danish royalty lived and conducted their business, and it remains a stunning example of Renaissance architecture and Danish history. As visitors approach the castle, they are immediately struck by its imposing façade, adorned with turrets and towers that rise above the landscape, as well as its location perched above the water, offering panoramic views of the strait and nearby Sweden. Inside the castle, visitors are transported back in time, wandering through opulent chambers, dark passageways, and the grand halls that once hosted royal banquets and important state matters. The iconic Hall of Knights, with its majestic wooden ceiling and intricate tapestries, leaves a lasting impression. The castle also features a fascinating museum that dives into its centuries-old history, with displays on its military role, royal lineage, and the artistic works that have shaped the castle's legacy, including Shakespeare's portrayal of the Danish royal family. One of the most captivating highlights of Kronborg Castle is the cellar, where the ghost of Holger Danske, a legendary Danish hero, is said to rest, awaiting the day when Denmark is in peril. Visitors can also explore the ramparts and take in the magnificent views of the Øresund Strait, which has played a significant role in Denmark's history. On a clear day, it is possible to spot the Swedish coastline from the castle, a reminder of the centuries-old rivalry between the two nations. The tranquil gardens surrounding the castle offer a perfect spot for a leisurely stroll, with the quiet murmur of the sea in the background providing a serene atmosphere.

Helsingør: Beyond the walls of Kronborg Castle, Helsingør itself is a delightful town that offers a blend of modernity and tradition. The town is easily walkable, with cobbled streets leading visitors to quaint shops, cozy cafés, and excellent restaurants that serve up traditional Danish fare. Helsingør is also home to other attractions, such as the Maritime Museum of Denmark, housed in a striking modern building near the castle, and the impressive St. Olaf's Church, whose soaring spire can be seen from miles around. A walk through Helsingør's harbor reveals charming boats bobbing gently in the water, and the area is ideal for a peaceful afternoon stroll. If you're looking for a local experience, you can visit the many fish markets along the waterfront, where fresh catches from the

Øresund Strait are sold daily. This coastal town exudes a relaxed atmosphere, providing a perfect contrast to the historical grandeur of Kronborg Castle.

Practical Tips for Visitors: When planning your trip to Helsingør and Kronborg Castle, it's important to note that the castle is open to visitors year-round, though hours of operation can vary depending on the season. Tickets to the castle generally cost around DKK 95 to DKK 135 (approximately 13-20 USD) for adults, with discounts available for students and children. If you wish to explore the castle with a guided tour, an additional fee may apply, but these tours are highly recommended for those seeking deeper insights into the history and legends of the castle. While the castle itself is a highlight, spending time in Helsingør also adds to the experience, as the town offers a welcoming atmosphere perfect for those who wish to immerse themselves in Danish coastal life. Given its proximity to Copenhagen, it's possible to easily combine a visit to Kronborg Castle with a day spent exploring Helsingør, offering a rich and fulfilling day of sightseeing. In terms of meals and dining options, Helsingør boasts a variety of choices ranging from quaint cafés where you can enjoy Danish pastries and coffee to more formal dining establishments that offer fresh seafood caught in the Øresund. Most visitors can expect to pay around DKK 100-200 (15-30 USD) for a casual meal, while a more upscale dining experience might cost a little more.

7.3 Hillerød and Frederiksborg Castle

One of the most enchanting day trips you can take from Copenhagen is a visit to Hillerød and its majestic Frederiksborg Castle. Located about 40 kilometers north of the Danish capital, Hillerød offers a blend of history, stunning architecture, and tranquil nature, all of which are encapsulated within the grandeur of Frederiksborg Castle. For those seeking an escape from the hustle and bustle of city life, this excursion provides the perfect balance of cultural immersion and scenic beauty.

Getting to Hillerød and Frederiksborg Castle from Copenhagen: Reaching Hillerød from Copenhagen is relatively simple, and the journey offers visitors a chance to experience Denmark's well-connected and efficient public transport system. Trains depart frequently from Copenhagen's central station, with the journey taking approximately 40 minutes. The cost for a one-way ticket typically ranges from 50 to 80 DKK (Danish Krone), depending on the time of day and class of service. The train ride itself is comfortable and offers picturesque views of the Danish countryside, providing a peaceful transition from the vibrant city to the more serene, historical town of Hillerød. Upon arriving at Hillerød Station, it is just a short walk—around 15 minutes—to reach Frederiksborg Castle. The path to the castle is lined with charming streets, and you may find yourself passing by quaint local shops and cafes, perfect for a quick break before diving into the history of the castle. Alternatively, local buses also operate and can bring visitors closer to the entrance.

Discovering Frederiksborg Castle: Frederiksborg Castle is the crown jewel of Hillerød and a must-visit for anyone with an interest in Danish history and architecture. As you approach the castle, it's impossible not to be awed by its fairy-tale appearance, sitting atop a small island in the middle of the castle lake. Built in the early 17th century by King Christian IV, Frederiksborg Castle was designed to be a symbol of the Danish monarchy's power and prestige. The castle's red brick walls, tall spires, and intricate carvings evoke a sense of regal grandeur that is felt upon entering its grounds. The castle is surrounded by lush, manicured gardens that provide a perfect setting for a leisurely stroll. Visitors can wander along the lake, through the parterres, and explore the expansive grounds, which offer stunning views of the castle from every angle. These gardens were meticulously designed and are a testament to the grand vision of their creators. The air is fresh, and the tranquil environment adds a layer of peaceful reflection to the whole experience.

The Castle's Interior and Museum: Inside the castle, you'll find an impressive array of rooms that have been preserved with remarkable detail, giving visitors a glimpse into Denmark's royal past. The castle houses the Museum of National History, which boasts a vast collection of paintings, furniture, and other artifacts dating from the Renaissance to the present day. One of the most captivating elements is the long corridors adorned with portraits of Danish kings and queens, offering a visual timeline of Denmark's royal heritage. Each room in the castle tells a different story, from the opulent royal chambers to the grand halls where the Danish court once gathered. The Chapel, with its intricate woodwork and golden details, stands as a symbol of the country's religious and cultural devotion. The castle's ballroom, on the other hand, reflects the splendor of Danish aristocracy and provides a window into the lavish parties and celebrations that once took place here. Visitors will also be drawn to the large collection of Dutch and Flemish paintings on display, which showcase the Renaissance's influence on Denmark. The museum's exhibits are not only a feast for the eyes but also offer fascinating insights into the lives of Denmark's royalty and the country's historical milestones.

Exploring the Surrounding Area: Once you've explored the castle and its museum, it's worth taking time to wander around the town of Hillerød itself. This charming town is known for its quaint streets and relaxed atmosphere. Many visitors enjoy stopping at one of the local cafes for a cup of coffee or perhaps a Danish pastry, a perfect treat after a day of sightseeing. The town is also home to several historical buildings and sites, including the Hillerød Church, which is situated close to the train station and worth a visit for its lovely architecture. For those with a bit more time on their hands, a walk through the surrounding countryside can provide a peaceful conclusion to your day trip. The area around Hillerød is dotted with lakes and woodlands, making it an ideal location for nature lovers. The nearby Store Dyrehave forest, just a short drive or bike ride from the town center, offers tranquil paths through woodlands, where you might spot deer and other wildlife.

Cost and Logistics: As for the cost, visitors should budget for the entrance fee to Frederiksborg Castle, which is approximately 125 DKK for adults. If you're traveling with children, the cost is often discounted, with many attractions offering free entry for younger visitors. The train ticket to Hillerød, as mentioned earlier, will add to the overall cost, but the experience is well worth the price. Additionally, if you're interested in exploring further, there may be additional costs for guided tours or museum exhibits.

7.4 Malmö and Sweden

Copenhagen offers a wealth of culture, history, and excitement. But for those who wish to venture beyond the Danish borders for a day, a trip to Malmö, Sweden's third-largest city, is an ideal escape. Located just across the Øresund Strait, Malmö is easily accessible from Copenhagen, making it a perfect destination for those looking to explore another Scandinavian gem. The journey from Copenhagen to Malmö takes about 40 minutes by train, covering a distance of roughly 35 kilometers (22 miles). This brief and seamless passage offers a wonderful opportunity to experience two distinct countries in one day.

Journey Across the Øresund Strait: To get to Malmö from Copenhagen, visitors can take a direct train from Copenhagen Central Station (København H), which runs regularly throughout the day. The train ride is comfortable and modern, with panoramic windows offering stunning views of the sea and the iconic Øresund Bridge, a feat of engineering that spans the strait and connects the two countries. Tickets for the train cost around 100-150 SEK (Swedish Krona) for a one-way journey, depending on the time and class of service. For those who prefer a more leisurely experience, buses are available as well, though they take a little longer, about 1 hour, and generally cost a bit less. Regardless of the mode of transportation, the journey is straightforward and allows for a smooth transition into Sweden, with no passport control between the two countries due to the Schengen Area agreement.

Arrival in Malmö: Once in Malmö, visitors are greeted by a city that blends modernity with a rich historical past. Malmö is a perfect mix of old and new, where medieval buildings stand side by side with cutting-edge contemporary architecture. As you step off the train, you're immediately immersed in the vibrancy of the city's cultural scene. Malmö Central Station is centrally located, offering easy access to the city's key attractions, including the striking Turning Torso, a twisting skyscraper that defines the city's skyline. The city's layout is pedestrian-friendly, and visitors can enjoy strolling through its charming streets, lined with cafes, boutiques, and galleries. A must-visit in Malmö is the picturesque Lilla Torg (Little Square), a cobblestone square surrounded by colorful buildings, restaurants, and lively outdoor seating areas. Here, visitors can enjoy a traditional Swedish fika (coffee break) at one of the cozy cafes or restaurants, where pastries like cinnamon buns are served with rich Swedish coffee. The square, with its relaxed ambiance, is an excellent spot to rest after wandering around the city. Malmö also boasts numerous parks and green spaces, with Kungsparken (King's Park) being one of the largest and most beautiful, perfect for a peaceful walk by the water or a boat ride on the canal.

Cultural and Culinary Delights: Malmö is also renowned for its culinary scene, influenced by both Scandinavian traditions and international flavors. The city's diverse population brings a unique fusion of cuisines, from Middle Eastern and Mediterranean to Asian and Latin American. A stroll through the Möllevången district, famous for its multicultural vibe, reveals an array of food markets and eateries where visitors can sample dishes from around the world. For a more traditional Swedish experience, visitors can indulge in Swedish meatballs served with lingonberry jam or try herring prepared in a variety of ways at one of Malmö's many seafood restaurants. One of the most striking features of Malmö is its commitment to sustainability and green living. The city is known for its environmental initiatives, and visitors can witness this firsthand by exploring areas such as the Western Harbour, a waterfront district that boasts eco-friendly buildings and a commitment to renewable energy. This area is also home to the Malmö City Library, an architectural marvel that is both a modern cultural hub and a testament to the city's environmental ethos.

Shopping and Leisure in Malmö: For those who enjoy shopping, Malmö offers a wide range of options. From designer boutiques in the city center to independent stores selling unique Scandinavian products, the city caters to all tastes. The Triangeln Shopping Center is a popular destination for those seeking a more commercial experience, offering everything from fashion and electronics to home goods. For a more relaxed shopping experience, Stortorget Square and its surroundings are perfect for leisurely browsing through local shops and markets. Additionally, Malmö's vibrant nightlife scene makes it an attractive destination for evening outings. Visitors can enjoy a night out in one of the city's chic cocktail bars or trendy nightclubs, which often feature live music performances or DJ sets. Malmö is known for its friendly atmosphere, and it's easy to find a place where locals and tourists mingle, making for an enjoyable and lively evening experience.

The Return Journey: As the day comes to an end, visitors can reflect on the memories made during their trip to Malmö. The journey back to Copenhagen is equally straightforward and relaxing, with regular train services running throughout the evening. As the train crosses the Øresund Bridge once again, it's a chance to take in the beauty of the Scandinavian landscape one last time. The city of Malmö offers a unique blend of history, culture, and modernity, all within a short distance of Copenhagen, making it a perfect destination for a day trip that combines the best of both Denmark and Sweden.

7.5 Louisiana Museum of Modern Art and Sculpture Park

Located just outside Copenhagen in the scenic town of Humlebæk, the Louisiana Museum of Modern Art is a must-visit for art lovers and anyone seeking a tranquil yet inspiring escape from the city. Renowned not only for its world-class collection of modern art but also for its stunning location overlooking the Øresund Strait, the Louisiana Museum offers an enriching blend of culture, nature, and architectural beauty. A day trip from Copenhagen to Louisiana promises a memorable experience, whether you're drawn to the artistic masterpieces within its walls or the serene landscapes of its sculpture park.

Transportation and Distance: The Louisiana Museum of Modern Art is situated around 35 kilometers north of Copenhagen, a convenient distance for a day trip. Visitors can easily reach the museum via public transportation, with the most popular option being the train. Departing from Copenhagen Central Station, a direct train ride to Humlebæk takes approximately 35 minutes. The train ride is scenic, as it passes through lush countryside and coastal views, providing a relaxing journey as you approach the museum. Once you arrive at Humlebæk Station, a short 10-minute walk will bring you to the Louisiana

Museum, allowing visitors to immerse themselves in the atmosphere of the area right from the start. For those preferring more flexibility, driving to the museum is also a great option. The drive takes around 40 minutes, depending on traffic, and provides a smooth route along the E47 highway. There are ample parking spaces available at the museum, making it easy for visitors to park and enjoy their visit without hassle. Whether by train or car, the journey to the Louisiana Museum is straightforward and provides the perfect opportunity to appreciate Denmark's charming landscape as you venture beyond the capital.

The Louisiana Museum of Modern Art: As one of Denmark's most iconic cultural institutions, the Louisiana Museum of Modern Art is a stunning place to explore the world of contemporary art. Founded in 1958, the museum is known for its exceptional collection of modern and contemporary art, featuring works by some of the biggest names in the art world, including Picasso, Andy Warhol, and Roy Lichtenstein, as well as pieces by Danish artists. The museum is constantly evolving, with new exhibitions showcasing both established and emerging artists. Visitors can expect to see a diverse range of art, from paintings and sculptures to installations and video art. The museum's architecture is equally impressive, with its minimalist design and large glass windows offering stunning views of the surrounding landscape. As you walk through the museum's galleries, you will be treated to a combination of thought-provoking art and breathtaking views of the natural surroundings. The Louisiana Museum's dedication to blending art with nature is evident in every corner of the museum, from its innovative exhibits to its seamless integration with the parkland outside.

One of the key features of the museum is its commitment to providing visitors with a dynamic, interactive experience. Temporary exhibitions are regularly featured, and these often focus on specific themes or movements within contemporary art. Whether it's a deep dive into the works of a particular artist or an exploration of a new artistic trend, each exhibition is carefully curated to engage visitors and spark conversation. The museum also offers educational programs, workshops, and guided tours for those who wish to deepen their understanding of the artworks on display.

The Sculpture Park: While the Louisiana Museum's interior is an artistic marvel, the museum's surrounding sculpture park is equally captivating. Spread out across a beautifully landscaped area, the park features an impressive collection of modern sculptures that blend harmoniously with the natural surroundings. The park is designed to encourage exploration, and as you wander through its pathways, you will encounter large-scale sculptures by famous artists such as Henry Moore, Alexander Calder, and Jean Arp. The open-air space of the sculpture park offers visitors the opportunity to engage with art in a more relaxed, immersive way. The sculptures are thoughtfully placed, often in locations that allow for the natural elements—such as the sea breeze and sunlight—to interact with the pieces, adding an additional layer of depth to the experience. The combination of art and nature creates an atmosphere of tranquility, allowing visitors to reflect on the pieces in a serene, contemplative setting. The sculpture park itself is expansive, and visitors are encouraged to spend time exploring the different sections, which are organized in ways that invite curiosity and discovery. Whether you choose to take a leisurely stroll or relax on one of the park's benches while taking in the view, the sculpture park offers a peaceful retreat, making it an ideal complement to the art within the museum.

Practical Information for Visitors: The Louisiana Museum is open daily, with hours typically from 11 AM to 6 PM. It is closed on certain holidays, so it is always a good idea to check their website for specific dates. The cost of admission is typically around DKK 130-160 ($20-25 USD) for adults, with discounted rates available for students, seniors, and children. Special exhibitions may have an additional fee, so it's worth checking ahead if there's something specific you wish to see. For transportation, a round-trip train ticket from Copenhagen to Humlebæk costs around DKK 70-100 ($10-15 USD), depending on the time of travel and available discounts.

CHAPTER 8
EVENTS AND FESTIVALS

8.1 Copenhagen Jazz Festival (July)

The Copenhagen Jazz Festival, held annually every July, is one of the most celebrated events in Denmark's vibrant cultural calendar. As the city transforms into a playground for music lovers, the festival invites both seasoned jazz enthusiasts and curious newcomers into a world where the rhythms of jazz take center stage. With over 1,000 concerts across various venues, ranging from cozy clubs to grand outdoor stages, the festival captures the essence of Copenhagen's creative spirit. It's an experience that not only celebrates music but also brings together a community of people from all over the world, uniting them in a shared love for the dynamic art form. The festival's history dates back to 1979, and since then, it has grown exponentially in both scale and reputation. From its humble beginnings, it has become one of the largest jazz festivals in Europe, attracting world-renowned artists, jazz legends, and rising stars. In July, the streets of Copenhagen pulse with the sounds of improvisation, experimentation, and jazz tradition. For anyone passionate about music, the Copenhagen Jazz Festival is a must-see event that promises an unforgettable experience.

A Musical Journey Across the City: What makes the Copenhagen Jazz Festival so unique is its ability to weave jazz seamlessly into the fabric of the city. As you stroll through the lively streets, you will encounter impromptu performances in parks, open-air spaces, and even on the canals. The festival is not confined to traditional concert halls but spreads across a range of unusual and diverse locations, creating an atmosphere where the music flows freely and unpredictably. Whether it's a spontaneous jam session on Nyhavn or a formal performance in one of Copenhagen's iconic venues, every corner of the city offers a different flavor of jazz. The festival's central hub, however, is the renowned Tivoli Gardens, where you can experience world-class performances under the stars. This venue, with its whimsical charm and beautifully illuminated surroundings, provides an enchanting backdrop for the festival's headline concerts. For a more intimate experience, many performances take place in smaller, historic jazz clubs like the famous Montmartre. These venues provide an authentic, up-close experience with the artists, allowing you to witness the improvisation and artistry of jazz in its most raw and spontaneous form.

Iconic Performances and International Talent: One of the greatest draws of the Copenhagen Jazz Festival is its ability to bring together some of the most talented jazz musicians from around the world. Each year, the lineup is a carefully curated mix of established jazz icons, cutting-edge experimental artists, and emerging talents. This blend ensures that there is something for every jazz lover, whether you are a fan of classic jazz, avant-garde sounds, or modern fusion. In 2025, expect to see performances from global jazz legends who have influenced generations of musicians, alongside thrilling collaborations between international stars and local Danish talent. With past performers including luminaries such as Herbie Hancock, Wayne Shorter, and Avishai Cohen, the festival continuously offers unforgettable moments for its audiences. For the true jazz connoisseur, this is an opportunity to witness once-in-a-lifetime performances, with some concerts being completely sold out within hours of their release. The excitement doesn't end with the headliners; throughout the festival, you can also discover new and up-and-coming artists who are pushing the boundaries of jazz. These performances, often held at more intimate venues or even open-air stages, offer the perfect opportunity for those looking to catch the next big thing in jazz before they hit the global stage.

The Atmosphere of Copenhagen in July: While the music is undoubtedly the star of the show, the Copenhagen Jazz Festival is also about immersing yourself in the unique atmosphere of the city in July. Copenhagen in summer is a beautiful sight, with its long daylight hours, mild weather, and vibrant outdoor culture. The jazz festival enhances this experience, with many performances taking place in open spaces where you can relax and enjoy the music with a drink in hand. Picture yourself sitting by the canals, the cool breeze ruffling your hair, as the sound of a smooth saxophone fills the air. For those who love to explore beyond the music, Copenhagen offers plenty of attractions to enjoy during your stay. Spend a day cycling through the city's scenic streets, exploring the historic Nyhavn district, or enjoying some world-class Danish cuisine at one of the city's trendy restaurants. The Copenhagen Jazz Festival, after all, is not just about listening to jazz—it's about being enveloped in the city's creative energy, and the festival's events allow you to do so while basking in the summer sun.

Practical Tips for Attending the Copenhagen Jazz Festival: To make the most of your experience at the Copenhagen Jazz Festival, planning ahead is essential. The festival typically runs for about 10 days in early July, with performances spread across different venues throughout the city. Many events are free, particularly those held in public spaces and outdoor locations. However, ticketed concerts, especially those in iconic venues like Tivoli Gardens or the Copenhagen Concert Hall, can sell out quickly, so securing tickets in advance is highly recommended. Getting around Copenhagen during the festival is relatively easy, as the city is well-known for its excellent public transportation system. You can take the metro, buses, or rent a bike to move between venues. The city is also very walkable, so you may find yourself discovering new concert venues just by wandering around. As for the entry fees, the cost of attending various performances varies. While many outdoor and street performances are free of charge, ticketed events usually range from around 100 DKK to 400 DKK, depending on the venue and the artist. It's always a good idea to check the festival's website for specific details on ticket availability and pricing, as well as to explore any free events or workshops that may be taking place.

8.2 Tivoli Gardens Christmas Market (December)

Every December, as Copenhagen's streets begin to sparkle with twinkling lights and the aroma of cinnamon fills the winter air, Tivoli Gardens transforms into a

Christmas market like no other. Located in the heart of the city, this festive destination is a must-visit for those looking to experience the true spirit of Christmas. With its enchanting atmosphere, filled with holiday cheer, Tivoli Gardens offers a unique opportunity to escape into a winter wonderland, where timeless traditions blend seamlessly with modern holiday delights. As you step into Tivoli Gardens during the holiday season, the first thing that strikes you is the transformation of this historic amusement park into a festive paradise. The Christmas market, open throughout the month of December, is a sensory feast: you'll find the cobblestone pathways lined with charming stalls selling everything from handcrafted toys and ornaments to gourmet treats and warm beverages. The twinkling lights adorning the trees, the soft glow of lanterns, and the delicate sounds of Christmas carols filling the air create a magical ambiance that is sure to delight visitors of all ages.

The Magic of the Christmas Market: The Tivoli Gardens Christmas Market is a celebration of everything that makes Christmas special. The market is a wonderful blend of Danish holiday traditions and global influences, showcasing a wide array of goods perfect for those seeking unique Christmas gifts or simply looking to immerse themselves in the holiday spirit. Stalls selling handcrafted candles, knitwear, and wooden toys are nestled beside those offering gourmet Danish treats like gløgg (mulled wine), roasted almonds, and the famous Danish æbleskiver (round doughnut-like pancakes), which are especially comforting in the cold December air. Tivoli Gardens has always been known for its impeccable attention to detail, and this is no different during the Christmas season. The park's gardens are beautifully decorated with thousands of sparkling lights, transforming Tivoli into a festive dreamscape. The shimmering trees and the famous Fountain of the Nymphs, with its gentle mist, create an idyllic setting for visitors to take a leisurely stroll, hand in hand with loved ones, enjoying the festive decorations and the magical ambiance.

Festive Entertainment and Performances: One of the highlights of the Tivoli Gardens Christmas Market is the entertainment on offer. Throughout December, the park hosts a variety of performances, from traditional Danish Christmas choirs to theatrical productions that capture the essence of the season. One of the most beloved performances is the "Tivoli Christmas Concert," where visitors can enjoy the enchanting sounds of a live orchestra performing Christmas carols in the stunning Tivoli Concert Hall. The concert hall itself, with its vintage charm and intimate atmosphere, offers the perfect setting for an evening of classical music that brings the holiday season to life. In addition to live music, Tivoli also offers magical light shows and festive parades, where costumed performers and towering snowmen move through the park, creating a whimsical atmosphere that enchants children and adults alike. The nightly illumination of Tivoli Gardens is nothing short of breathtaking, with lights twinkling in every corner of the park. The sight of the entire park bathed in a soft, golden glow against the backdrop of the cold winter night is something that will stay with you long after your visit.

Visiting Tivoli Gardens Christmas Market: Tivoli Gardens is easily accessible from Copenhagen's city center, making it a convenient destination for locals and tourists alike. The park is located just a short walk from the main train station, Copenhagen Central Station (Hovedbanegården), and is well-connected by public transportation, including buses and the Metro. Visitors can also take a leisurely walk through Copenhagen's charming streets to reach the park, soaking in the festive atmosphere along the way. The Christmas market typically opens at the beginning of November and runs until just after Christmas, with the most magical moments happening throughout December. For those planning to visit Tivoli during the Christmas season, it's important to note that the park can become quite busy, particularly on weekends and during the lead-up to Christmas. Therefore, it's recommended to arrive early in the day or visit on a weekday to avoid the largest crowds.

8.3 Copenhagen Pride and Parade (August)

Copenhagen, a city known for its open-mindedness and inclusivity, is a global beacon for LGBTQ+ rights and celebrations, with its Copenhagen Pride standing as one of the largest and most vibrant events in Scandinavia. Every August, the city transforms into a kaleidoscope of rainbow colors, music, love, and equality, attracting thousands of visitors from all around the world to join in this powerful week-long celebration. Whether you are an ally, a member of the LGBTQ+ community, or simply someone seeking to be a part of something extraordinary, Copenhagen Pride is an experience that leaves an indelible mark on the soul.

A Celebration of Diversity: Held every year in August, Copenhagen Pride is not just a parade or a series of events; it is a movement for social change, a loud and proud declaration of love, equality, and acceptance. It is a time when the city comes alive with the energy of people from all walks of life, uniting under the shared belief that everyone deserves to live authentically and freely. The event is not merely about revelry; it's a passionate demonstration for the rights of the LGBTQ+ community, a call to action for equal treatment, and a celebration of the victories that have been achieved while acknowledging the ongoing struggles that still exist. Copenhagen Pride is a chance for people to come together in solidarity, to spread awareness, and to be a part of something greater than themselves. Its atmosphere is both jubilant and poignant, inviting participants to reflect on the importance of the message it carries while immersing themselves in an unforgettable festival of color, music, and togetherness. Whether you find yourself marching alongside thousands of others during the Pride Parade or attending one of the many cultural events and parties, every moment feels like a step forward in the march for equality.

The Pride Parade: The crowning jewel of Copenhagen Pride is the Pride Parade, which typically takes place on the Saturday of the festival week, in mid-August. This parade is not only a visual feast but a celebration of courage and visibility. Thousands of people, from locals to international visitors, don their most vibrant outfits and march through the heart of Copenhagen, with music, floats, and joyful dancing filling the streets. The parade is an emotionally charged spectacle that weaves through the city's most iconic streets, such as Frederiksberggade and Vesterbro, creating a stunning visual representation of love in all its forms. The atmosphere is electric, charged with a sense of freedom and acceptance. Visitors who attend can join in the parade or line the streets to cheer on the participants, feeling the infectious energy and sense of unity that defines the event. This parade is not only about self-expression but also about sending a powerful message to the world: Copenhagen is a city that celebrates its differences and champions equality for all.

Pride Week: While the Pride Parade is undoubtedly the highlight, Copenhagen Pride encompasses a full week of events, celebrations, and educational activities that cater to all interests. Throughout the week, Copenhagen's iconic squares, parks, and venues play host to a variety of performances, talks, and cultural experiences that invite people to explore LGBTQ+ history, art, and politics. These events are open to all, making it a celebration of diversity in its truest sense. The Pride Week includes art exhibitions, live music performances, film screenings, and discussions on LGBTQ+ issues that are both informative and empowering. One of the most anticipated events is the annual Pride Garden, held in the beautiful Frederiksberg Gardens, where visitors can relax and enjoy a peaceful, family-friendly atmosphere amidst the hustle and bustle of the city. The Pride Garden offers an opportunity to connect with others, learn more about LGBTQ+ advocacy, and enjoy live performances by local artists. For those with a passion for film, the Copenhagen Pride Film Festival is a must-attend. Showcasing an array of LGBTQ+ films from around the globe, the festival provides a space for filmmakers and audiences to connect over thought-provoking and poignant stories. It is a perfect blend of entertainment and education, ensuring that everyone, regardless of their background, can engage with important LGBTQ+ narratives.

Pride Week Parties: When the sun sets on Copenhagen, the celebration continues into the night with an exciting array of Pride parties and events that span the city's diverse nightlife scene. From intimate gatherings in underground bars to massive club events, Copenhagen's Pride parties are legendary for their inclusivity and non-stop energy. One of the most iconic events during Pride Week is the official Pride Party, held in the stunning Forum Copenhagen. This event attracts international DJs, celebrities, and thousands of revelers who dance the night away to the beat of the latest tunes. It's a fantastic opportunity to meet like-minded people, celebrate the LGBTQ+ community, and experience

8.4 Copenhagen Marathon and Running Events (May)

Among the most anticipated of these events is the Copenhagen Marathon, a celebration of endurance, sportsmanship, and the joy of running. Held every year in May, this marathon is one of the most prominent running events in Europe, attracting both seasoned athletes and enthusiastic amateurs. But the marathon itself is just one of several events that take place during this dynamic month, where runners can partake in various challenges that not only test their physical limits but also immerse them in the beauty and energy of Copenhagen.

The Copenhagen Marathon: Taking place in May, the Copenhagen Marathon is undoubtedly the centerpiece of the city's running events. This race, renowned for its flat, fast course, offers participants an opportunity to experience the city in a truly unique way. The route weaves through Copenhagen's most iconic districts, from the lively streets of Vesterbro to the historic Christianshavn, and past the serene waters of Kastellet and Langelinie. What makes this marathon truly special is how it captures the essence of Copenhagen—combining modernity with history, tranquility with urban energy. Runners are treated not only to the thrill of racing but also to the beauty of the city, which is often overlooked by the typical tourist. The marathon attracts runners of all abilities, from elite athletes gunning for personal records to those looking to complete their first marathon. The event's festive atmosphere ensures that everyone feels welcome. Spectators line the streets, cheering on the participants, creating an electric energy that makes the entire experience unforgettable. The race begins in the heart of the city and spans 42.195 kilometers, offering a thrilling challenge for those with the stamina and determination to cross the finish line. Getting to the Copenhagen Marathon is straightforward. The start and finish lines are centrally located near Fælledparken, making it easily accessible by public transport. Copenhagen's excellent metro and bus systems connect the marathon route with many parts of the city, ensuring that both participants and visitors can easily navigate the area. The entry fee for the event typically ranges from 60 to 120 EUR, depending on the registration date. Early registrants often enjoy discounted rates, while late entries may pay a premium. Participants are encouraged to register in advance through the official marathon website to secure a spot in the race.

The Royal Run: In addition to the marathon, May also brings another exciting event to Copenhagen—the Royal Run, a unique running event that was introduced in 2018 to celebrate Denmark's royal family. This event is more than just a race; it's an embodiment of Danish unity and pride. The Royal Run allows participants to run or walk alongside members of the Danish royal family, adding an extraordinary touch to the experience. The event includes a variety of race distances, ranging from a 1.8 km family run to a 10 km race for those looking for more of a challenge. What sets the Royal Run apart is the opportunity to share the course with Denmark's crown prince, Crown Prince Frederik, who has often been seen participating in the event himself. The Royal Run typically takes place on Pentecost Monday, which in May offers perfect spring weather. The event spans across several cities, with Copenhagen being one of the key host locations. Participants can enjoy a scenic course that takes them through the city's famous parks and picturesque streets, all while feeling the pulse of the royal celebration. The event encourages inclusivity, making it an excellent choice for families, beginners, and experienced runners alike. There's no better way to feel connected to Copenhagen's spirit of togetherness than by participating in this one-of-a-kind event. The Royal Run's central start area is located near the iconic Amalienborg Palace, the residence of the Danish royal family, adding an extra layer of grandeur to the occasion. With the participation of the royal family members, the event draws large crowds, ensuring an unforgettable atmosphere. Entry fees for the Royal Run are usually modest, ranging between 25 and 50 EUR, depending on the distance and the timing of registration. Visitors can easily reach the start area via Copenhagen's efficient public transport system.

The Night Marathon: For those looking for a unique twist on the traditional marathon experience, the Copenhagen Night Marathon offers an unforgettable challenge. As the name suggests, this marathon is held in the evening, offering a different perspective of the city under the glow of streetlights and city lights. The route takes runners through some of Copenhagen's most scenic areas, including Tivoli Gardens, which is beautifully illuminated at night, and past the sparkling waters of the Copenhagen Harbour. The nighttime marathon offers a serene and atmospheric experience, as the cool evening air and quieter streets make for a more reflective and meditative race. Participants often remark on how the night setting brings a sense of magic and tranquility to the race. While this event isn't held as frequently as the traditional marathon, when it does take place, it's an exceptional experience that stands apart from the usual daytime races. The Night Marathon usually takes place in May and attracts a diverse crowd, from elite runners to those simply seeking a memorable night out. The event has become increasingly popular in recent years, with many runners taking advantage of the cooler temperatures to push their limits. The entry fee typically ranges between 50 and 80 EUR, with registration available online well in advance.

The Copenhagen 5K: For those who may find a full marathon too daunting but still wish to participate in Copenhagen's running events, the Copenhagen 5K is an ideal choice. This event, typically held alongside the marathon in May, offers a more relaxed yet still rewarding experience. The 5K course is shorter, but no less scenic, taking participants through some of the city's most beautiful streets, with views of the iconic Nyhavn harbor, Amalienborg Palace, and lush green spaces. The event is perfect for newcomers to running, families, or those looking for a fun challenge without the intensity of a longer race. The Copenhagen 5K emphasizes the joy of running rather than competitive performance, and it's a wonderful way to experience the city's energetic atmosphere. Whether you're running for fitness, fun, or to celebrate the city itself, the 5K ensures a supportive, friendly environment for all. With an entry fee that typically sits around 30 to 40 EUR, it remains an affordable and accessible option for those looking to partake in one of Copenhagen's most popular running events.

Copenhagen Running Festival: In addition to the competitive events, May also sees the Copenhagen Running Festival, a celebration of fitness, health, and the running community. This event spans several days, featuring a variety of races for different skill levels, including fun runs, 10Ks, and half marathons. The festival aims to bring people together to share their passion for running, with runners of all ages and abilities encouraged to participate. It's an ideal event for those who wish to combine their love of running with the social experience of a fitness festival. The Copenhagen Running Festival often includes health and fitness expos, where visitors can learn about the latest in running technology, gear, and nutrition. It's a great opportunity to meet like-minded individuals and connect with fellow runners, all while enjoying the beautiful Copenhagen backdrop. With an entry fee ranging from 30 EUR for shorter distances to 80 EUR for half marathons, the festival offers a range of price points to suit different budgets. Copenhagen in May is a city alive with the energy of athletes and fitness enthusiasts, and the running events provide an unforgettable way to experience the city. Whether you're aiming for the full marathon challenge, participating in a family fun run, or simply looking to enjoy the festive atmosphere, Copenhagen's May running events offer something for everyone.

8.5 Strøget Christmas Lights and Shopping (December)

As December rolls around, Copenhagen transforms into a winter wonderland, with festive lights illuminating the city streets, creating a magical atmosphere that enchants both locals and visitors alike. Among the city's most renowned holiday experiences is the Strøget Christmas Lights and Shopping event. Strøget, the bustling pedestrian street stretching across the heart of Copenhagen, becomes a shining symbol of the city's holiday spirit. Visitors flock to this iconic street not only to admire its dazzling Christmas lights but also to immerse themselves in the unique shopping experience that combines tradition and modernity. Held every December, Strøget Christmas Lights and Shopping brings the holiday season to life with a perfect blend of visual spectacle and retail delight. From the moment you step onto the cobbled streets of Strøget, you are greeted by a fairy-tale atmosphere, where the shimmering lights reflect off the historic buildings and the air is filled with the scent of mulled wine and roasted almonds. This event offers more than just a typical shopping experience; it is a celebration of Copenhagen's unique approach to the holiday season, showcasing both traditional Danish Christmas charm and contemporary European style.

A Stroll Through Strøget: One of the most enchanting features of the Strøget Christmas Lights and Shopping event is the spectacular display of holiday lights that adorn the entire shopping district. The street itself becomes a living canvas, with thousands of twinkling lights decorating the trees, shop windows, and facades of the historic buildings that line the street. The atmosphere is nothing short of magical, as visitors walk beneath a canopy of golden lights that stretch from one end of Strøget to the other. The entire stretch from City Hall Square to Kongens Nytorv is transformed into a dazzling spectacle that beckons both shoppers and admirers. As you wander along Strøget, you'll pass by elaborately decorated windows showcasing the latest fashion trends, traditional Danish Christmas ornaments, and a wide variety of unique gifts perfect for the holiday season. The windows themselves are often works of art, with intricate displays that tell stories of Christmas traditions and Copenhagen's history. Whether it's the charming decorations of the iconic department store Magasin du Nord or the upscale boutiques along the street, each window along Strøget adds to the festive atmosphere that envelops you.

Copenhagen's Christmas Markets: While the Christmas lights are undeniably mesmerizing, Strøget Christmas Lights and Shopping is equally about the experience of holiday shopping in one of Europe's most charming retail districts. Throughout December, Strøget is home to a variety of Christmas markets, each offering a diverse selection of festive goods. The market stalls are beautifully set up, offering everything from handmade Christmas ornaments to Danish delicacies, such as Æbleskiver (Danish pancakes) and Gløgg (mulled wine). Visitors can wander from stall to stall, sipping on hot chocolate or mulled wine while browsing for unique holiday gifts. The markets around Strøget are particularly known for their high-quality local products, such as Danish design items, artisanal crafts, and gourmet treats. For those looking to take home a piece of Copenhagen's holiday spirit, the markets are the perfect place to find beautifully crafted wooden toys, woolen scarves, and traditional Danish porcelain. These are not just souvenirs, but pieces of the local culture that capture the warmth and tradition of a Copenhagen Christmas.

Ice Skating at Frederiksberg Runddel: For those seeking a bit of outdoor fun during their Strøget Christmas Lights and Shopping experience, the ice skating rink at Frederiksberg Runddel offers a perfect festive activity. Located just a short walk from Strøget, this popular ice rink provides a picturesque setting for both novice skaters and seasoned pros. The rink is surrounded by festive lights, with the historic Frederiksberg Gardens providing a beautiful backdrop. Skating here is a magical experience, especially as the rink is nestled in one of the city's most beautiful park areas, surrounded by trees lit up with twinkling lights. Skating under the stars, with the soft glow of lanterns illuminating the area, adds an extra layer of enchantment to the Copenhagen Christmas experience. Entry fees for the ice rink are relatively affordable, and rentals for skates are available on-site. Whether you are looking to have fun with friends or enjoy a romantic moment with a loved one, ice skating at Frederiksberg Runddel is a holiday activity that fits perfectly with the festive spirit of the season.

Holiday Concerts and Performances at Strøget: Copenhagen's Strøget Christmas Lights and Shopping event goes beyond just shopping and light displays; it is also a celebration of music and culture. During December, various musical performances and holiday concerts take place throughout the city, many of which can be found around Strøget. These performances feature choirs singing traditional Danish Christmas carols, live jazz bands, and even classical ensembles playing festive favorites. One of the most notable venues for such performances is the historic St. Nicholas' Church (Sankt Nikolaj Kirke), where visitors can enjoy candlelit concerts in a stunning Baroque setting.

CONCLUSION AND RECOMMENDATIONS

As your journey through Copenhagen comes to a close, it's clear that this city offers far more than the picturesque views, vibrant culture, and rich history often showcased in brochures. The true magic of Copenhagen lies in its soul—the charming, laid-back rhythm of the city, the seamless blend of old-world architecture with cutting-edge modernity, and the feeling of being embraced by a community that takes pride in its sustainability, its culinary scene, and its welcoming atmosphere. Copenhagen is not just a place to visit, it's a city that beckons you to live in the moment. From strolling along the cobblestone streets of Nyhavn to soaking up the creative energy of the trendy Vesterbro district, every corner invites you to experience something unique. And yet, Copenhagen's appeal isn't just in its obvious beauty—it's in the hidden gems, the small details, and the experiences that reveal themselves only to those who venture off the beaten path. It's the kind of city that rewards the curious traveler, those willing to immerse themselves in the local way of life. Now, as you prepare to embark on your own Copenhagen adventure, here are some insider tips to make the most of your time in this captivating city. These nuggets of wisdom will not only elevate your trip but will also help you uncover Copenhagen like a local.

Insider Tips to Unlock the Best of Copenhagen

Go Beyond the Tourist Traps: While spots like Tivoli Gardens and The Little Mermaid are iconic and worth visiting, take the time to explore Copenhagen's lesser-known treasures. Head to the vibrant district of Nørrebro, where you can wander through eclectic shops, sip coffee in cozy cafes, and enjoy delicious Middle Eastern dishes in local restaurants. This area pulses with multicultural energy, a far cry from the polished tourist centers.

Embrace Copenhagen's Cycling Culture: Copenhagen is renowned for being one of the world's most bike-friendly cities. Don't just walk—rent a bike and become a part of the city's cycling culture. Ride along the harbor, past the colorful houses of Nyhavn, and through the green spaces of Frederiksberg Have. The local bike paths are well-maintained, and cycling offers a more intimate way to experience the city's pulse.

Dine Like a Local: Copenhagen's culinary scene is a feast for the senses, and while Michelin-starred restaurants like Noma may get all the attention, the true essence of Danish cuisine lies in the cozy neighborhood spots. Look for smørrebrød—open-faced sandwiches that are a national staple, or dive into a Danish pastry at one of the local bakeries, like Lagkagehuset. If you're feeling adventurous, try a Danish hot dog, sold from iconic street carts all over the city.

Visit Local Markets for Authentic Souvenirs: Skip the typical souvenir shops and head to Torvehallerne, Copenhagen's bustling food market, for a taste of local life. Here, you'll find fresh Danish produce, artisanal cheeses, homemade jams, and pastries that make the perfect souvenir or picnic snack. This is the place to pick up unique, locally-made gifts like handcrafts or Danish-designed home goods that you won't find anywhere else.

Find Tranquility in the City's Green Spaces: Copenhagen is blessed with an abundance of green spaces that are perfect for a quiet escape from the city hustle. The King's Garden is a peaceful spot to unwind, and the lesser-known Superkilen Park in Nørrebro is an urban oasis filled with art installations and cultural symbols from around the world. Whether you're enjoying a relaxed afternoon or having a picnic with a view, these parks provide the perfect setting to experience Copenhagen's slower pace.

Visit the Local Galleries and Art Spaces: Copenhagen is a city of creativity, and its art scene goes far beyond the famed National Gallery. Discover local art in unconventional spaces like Copenhagen Contemporary, a vast exhibition space housed in a former industrial building, or the Art of Copenhagen tour, which showcases street art that's hidden in plain sight around the city. These artistic experiences will introduce you to the city's modern artistic soul.

Copenhagen is a city that invites you to explore, discover, and get lost in its charm. Whether you are basking in the vibrant colors of the city's streets, savoring a meal at a hidden restaurant, or simply enjoying the peacefulness of one of its many parks, Copenhagen offers something unique for every type of traveler. With these insider tips, you're not just visiting Copenhagen—you're immersing yourself in its essence, discovering its secrets, and creating memories that will last a lifetime.

Printed in Great Britain
by Amazon